C000002606

Florence

MICHELIN
Travel Publications

CONTENTS

t is not easy to explain the complexity of feelings aroused when one visits the city, be it for the first time or the hundredth. Florence is known to be a prestigious city of art which has nurtured men of genius and is the birthplace of the Italian language and the cradle of humanistic civilization. Visitors may have a long wait before gaining admission to admire Boticelli's Venus, and the city's narrow streets are ill-suited to dense traffic. The *Arno,* where the writer Manzoni used to "wash his linen", is described as the mirror in which Florence looks at herself each morning to make sure that she is still the fairest in the land, even though lately, the river has wounded and bruised her. In spite of all these factors, the beauty of Florence is beyond compare as the city exerts its seductive charms anew. ■

B. Juge/MICHELIN

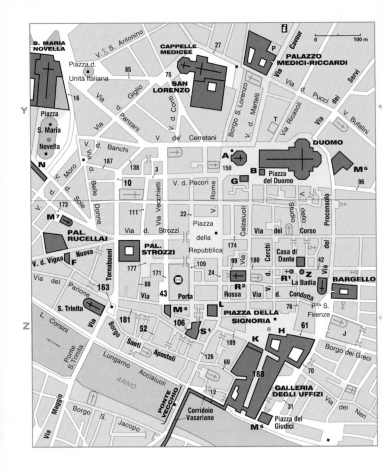

11

Not to be Missed

Florence has such an abundance of works of art that visitors may feel overwhelmed and lose their sense of direction; they may also find it difficulty to select the sites to visit and feel tired from walking all day and from the dense traffic.

Visitors who do not want to miss the "must see" sights should visit the following:

Piazza del Duomo★★★

Galleria degli Uffizi★★★

Palazzo Vecchio★★★

Masterpieces★★★ by Michelangelo in the Galleria dell'Accademia

Museo del Bargello★★★

San Lorenzo and Tombe Medicee★★★

Galleria Palatina★★★ in Palazzo Pitti

Masterpieces★★★ by Beato Angelico in the Museo di San Marco

Frescoes★★★ by Ghirlandaio in Santa Maria Novella

Frescoes★★★ by Masolino, Masaccio and Filippino Lippi in the Cappella Brancacci, in San Spirito

Frescoes by Benozzo Gozzoli★★★ in Palazzo Medici-Riccardi

BACKGROUND

IN THE BEGINNING

The colony of Florentia was founded in the IC BC by Julius Caesar on the north bank of the Arno at a spot level with the Ponte Vecchio. It was only in the early IIC that the city became an important Tuscan centre when Count Ugo, Marquis of Tuscany, took up residence here, and again towards the end of the same century when the Countess Matilda affirmed its independence.

During the I2C Florence prospered under the influence of the new class of merchants. This period saw the rise of trades organised in powerful guilds *(arti)*, which soon became the ruling class when Florence became an

Internal Strife – Guelphs and Ghibellines

The economic "miracle" was all the more amazing given the violent feuds that raged not only between Florence and other major towns in Tuscany but also between various Florentine factions within the city.

It was in the 13C that the Guelphs, supporters of the Pope, and the Ghibellines, supporters of the Holy Roman Emperor, first appeared on the scene. At first the Guelphs were victorious but the Ghibellines set up alliances with other cities that were opposed to Florence, in particular with Siena, and defeated the Guelphs at Montaperti in 1260. The Guelphs regained their strength and in 1266 they returned to Florence and made considerable changes in the city centre since they systematically demolished the many Ghibelline tower-house. Under the Guelphs the city became a republic with a democratic constitution ruled from the Palazzo Vecchio by a government mainly composed of representatives *(Priori)* of the guilds. Divisions then began to appear between Black and White Guelphs; the latter broke away from the Papacy. Owing to this tragic development, Dante, a member of the White Guelph faction, was banished for life from his native city in January 1302. In 1348 the Black Death killed more than one-half of the population of Florence and put an end to internal strife.

One of the residences of the Medici:
Villa Poggio a Caiano

independent commune. These tradesmen were ably supported by the Florentine money houses which succeeded the Lombard and Jewish institutions, and themselves acquired a great reputation by issuing the first-ever bills of exchange and the famous florin, struck with the Florentine coat of arms. The latter was replaced in the late 15C by the Venetian ducat.

Despite its prosperity, Florence did not escape the internal strife between the Ghibellines who were partisans of the Holy Roman Emperor and the Guelphs who supported the Pope.

Among the numerous wealthy families in Florence, it was the **Medici** who gave the city several leaders who exercised their patronage both in the sphere of fine arts and finance.

Lorenzo the Magnificent (1449-92) the most famous of all the Medici. He was a highly intelligent but not a handsome man. Although he was only 20 when his father died, he began to direct the affairs of Florence, but covertly, in accordance with the family tradition. He was less discreet than his predecessors, ruling like a prince and exercising personal power. He was outstanding for his skilful diplomacy and, like his grandfather, he succeeded in maintaining the dominant position of Florence in Italy and the balance of power between the Papacy and the various States; he was likened to the pointer on a set of scales (ago della bilancia). On the other hand, he proved to be less than able in managing the commercial and banking business bequeathed to him by his

Savonarola (1452-98)

The Dominican monk from Ferrara who became prior of St Mark's monastery, was to cause the downfall of the Medici by taking advantage of a difficult period when Florentines were faced with crumbling republican institutions and France and Spain were at war, each struggling for control of Europe as a whole. The fanatical, ascetic monk was the complete antithesis of ordinary Florentines, who had a deep love of the arts and life in general. Yet they submitted to his power in 1493, when he preached a terrifying and powerful sermon from the pulpit of the cathedral, denouncing the pleasures of the senses and love of the arts.

father, and this led to the ruin of the financial empire of the Medici. He was less generous than his father and grandfather, particularly in his **treatment of the Pazzi**. He was a fascinating character, a combination of hedonism and political realism, cold calculation and intransigence, yet a man with enormous artistic and humanistic sensitivity, a supreme example of Renaissance man. He was a lover of the arts and a talented writer of verse; his friends – the painters, philosophers and poets who made up his court – were on familiar terms with him and called him Lauro (laurel bush).

On Lorenzo's death, which had repercussions throughout Europe, the Dominican monk **Girolamo Savonarola**, taking advantage of a period of confusion, provoked the fall of the Medici.

The Medici family returned to power with the help of the Emperor Charles V and they reigned until the mid-18C. After the Medici, the Grand Duchy passed to the House of Lorraine, then to Napoleon Bonaparte until 1814 before returning to the House of Lorraine until 1859.

When it became part of the Italian Kingdom, Florence was capital from 1865 to 1870. ■

A MIRACLE OF GRACE AND GENIUS

The main characteristics of the greatest movement in Florentine culture, which was later to be known as the Renaissance, were partly a receptivity to the outside world, a dynamic open-minded attitude, and partly a desire to achieve universality which resulted in a multiplication of the fields of interest. Dante was not only a great poet but also a grammarian and historian who did much research on the origins and versatility of his own language. He was one of Florence's most active polemicists. Giotto was not only a painter but also an architect. Lorenzo the Magnificent was the prince who best incarnated the spirit of the Renaissance: an able diplomat, a realistic politician, a patron of the arts as well as a poet himself. This quest to achieve a balance between nature and order had its most brilliant exponent in Michelangelo, painter, architect, sculptor and scholar whose work typifies a purely Florentine preoccupation.

Moreover, Florence is set in the heart of a serenely beautiful **countryside***** which is bathed

The incomparable delicacy of Botticelli

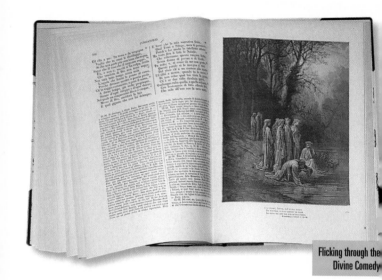

by a soft, amber light. Florentine architects and artists have variously striven to recreate this natural harmony in their works.

The relatively late emergence of Florence in the 11C as a cultural centre and its insignificant Roman heritage no doubt contributed to the growth of an independent art movement, which developed vigorously for several centuries. One of its principal characteristics was its preoccupation with clarity and harmony which influenced writers as well as architects, painters and sculptors.

Dante Alighieri (1265-1321), a supporter of the White Guelf faction which broke away from the Papacy, played an active part in the politics of Florence. In 1302 he was forced into exile by his opponents, the Black Guelfs, and spent the remainder of his life travelling throughout Italy until he died in Ravenna.

Author of Vita Nuova (New Life), in which he recounts his love for Beatrice, *Rime*, Convivio (The Banquet) and De vulgari eloquentia (Concerning Vernacular Eloquence),

His masterpiece, the *Divine Comedy,* is an allegorical poem describing his journey beyond the grave. Guided by Virgil in Hell and in Purgatory, and by Beatrice in Paradise, Dante meets many dead people, some damned and some among the chosen. Their sufferings or joys are proportionate to their behaviour during their time on Earth.

Botticelli (1444-1510)

Botticelli was a pupil of Filippo Lippi and later Verrocchio; he was also an admirer of Pollaiolo. All three artists had a great influence on Botticelli who retained the linearity and contour of Lippi, while showing, in his work, the energy characteristic of the other two. He remained indifferent, however, to the introduction of atmosphere into painting that Verrocchio had begun to explore. By the end of the 15C he was the greatest painter in Florence – he was among the artists called to Rome to paint the walls of the Sistine Chapel – and he mixed with the circle of neo-Platonist scholars, philosophers and writers at the court of Lorenzo the Magnificent, a great admirer of this artist. He revived the themes of Antiquity and painted mythological subjects – Venus, Pallas and the Centaur, Primavera (Spring) – bringing to them a tender lyricism that gave them an allegorical quality. He also painted numerous Madonnas and he excelled in introducing a sense of movement and rhythm to fabrics, veils, hair and limbs. The faces of his subjects are tilted rather systematically to one side in a somewhat Mannerist style. The death of Lorenzo the Magnificent, the preaching of Savonarola and the future development of his artistic style, which through its exaggerated curves bordered on an affectation of the Gothic style, all conspired to push the artist from a state of extreme sensitivity to open doubt, as is shown in his *Calumny of Apelles,* a work drawn in such an incisive way that it arouses a feeling of distress. Although he embodies all that was best during the finest years of the century of the Medici, Botticelli failed to influence other artists because his originality was difficult to emulate.

Niccolò Machiavelli (1469-1527), born in Florence, was the statesman on whose account Machiavellism became a synonym for cunning; he recounted his experiences as a statesman in a noble and vigorous prose. He was the author of The Prince (*Il Principe* – 1513), an essay on political science and government dedicated to Lorenzo II in which he counselled that in politics the end justifies the means.

Francesco Guicciardini (1483-1540) wrote an important history of Florence and Italy, while **Giorgio Vasari** (1511-74), much later, with his work *The Lives of the Most Eminent Italian Architects, Painters and Sculptors,* was the first real art historian. He studied and classified local schools of painting, tracing their development from the 13C with the work of Cimabue.

The Florentine school had its origins in the work of **Cimabue** (1240-1302) and slowly it freed itself from the Byzantine tradition with its decorative convolutions,

cello (1397-1475), **Andrea de Castagno** (1423-57), **Piero della Francesca** a native of the Marche who were all ardent exponents in the matters of foreshortening and the strictly geometrical construction of space; while others such as **Fra Angelico** (1387-1455), and later **Filippo Lippi** (1406-69) and **Benozzo Gozzoli** (1420-97) were imbued with the traditions of International Gothic and were more concerned with the visual effects of arabesques and the appeal of

while **Giotto** (1266-1337) in his search for truth gave priority to movement and expression. Later **Masaccio** (1401-28) studied spatial dimension and modelling. From then on perspective became the principal preoccupation of Florentine painters, sculptors, architects and theorists who continually tried to perfect this technique. The Quattrocento (15C) saw the emergence of a group of artists like **Paolo Uc-**

luminous colours. These opposing tendencies were reconciled in the harmonious balance of the work of **Sandro Botticelli** (1444-1510) He took his subjects from Antiquity and he invented fables peopled by enigmatic figures with subtle linear forms, which created an impression of tension. At times a certain melancholy seems to arrest the movement and dim the luminosity of the colours.

Alongside Botticelli, the **Pollaiolo** brothers, **Domenico Ghirlandaio** (1449-94) and **Filippino Lippi** (1457-1504) ensure the continuity and diversity of Florentine art. The High Renaissance with its main centres in Rome and other northern towns reached Florence in the 16C. **Leonardo da Vinci**, **Michelangelo** and **Raphael**, all made their debut at Florence, and inspired younger Mannerist artists such as **Jacopo Pontormo**, **Rosso Fiorentino**, **Andrea del Sarto**

constant preoccupation was with perspective in the arrangement of interiors and the design of façades. **Leon Battista Alberti** (1404-72) was the theorist and grand master of such a movement. However it was **Filippo Brunelleschi** (1377-1446) who best represented the Florentine spirit, and he gave the city buildings which combined both rigour and grace.

At the end of the century, owing to the political upheavals following the death of Lorenzo the Magnifi-

The guild system of late 13C Florence divided crafts and professions into seven "major trades" (shown here), five "middle trades" and nine "minor trades"

(1486-1530) and the curious portraitist of the Medici, **Agnolo Bronzino** (1503-72).

The emergence of a Florentine school of painting is, however, indissociable from the contemporary movement of the architects who were creating a style, also inspired by Antiquity, which united the classical traditions of rhythm, a respect for proportion and geometric decoration. The

cent, Florence entered a period of uncertainty which was perfectly translated by the passionate personality of **Michelangelo**, who combined pride and agony in his work. In his sculptures, as in his paintings, he achieved great realism; he surpassed the best of his predecessors, who produced merely probable personalised figures. Michelangelo's creations seem to be throbbing with inner life; the weight of their limbs and the strength of their muscles seem to be those of real people captured at a precise moment in time rather than set against the gentle timelessness of the perfect beauty favoured during the Renaissance. Examples of his genius include his proud *David (original in the Galleria dell'Accademia)*, his drunken *Bacchus (in the Bargello)*, his gentle *Virgin Mary and Staircase (in the Casa Buonarroti)* or his *Pietà (in the Museo dell'Opera del Duomo)*.

In architecture also, he breathed life into space by revolutionising the formalism of the Classical repertory – he divided up pediments and included empty niches in the new sacristy in San Lorenzo. In the entrance hall to the Laurenziana Library, he set columns into the walls, supporting them on flute brackets, treated the internal wall as if they were external and designed the staircase in three part so that it occupied almost a the floor space. He appropriate Brunelleschi's techniques – high lighting structural elements with *pietra serena,* a taste for centred designs, unification of volume – bu used them only to give greate freedom to the dynamics of space in which the old vocabulary is only a tool rather than a rigid means of achieving harmony.

Later **Benvenuto Cellini** (1500 71), Giambologna or **Giovanni Bologna** (1529-1608) and **Bartolomeo Ammannati** (1511-92) maintained this unity of style which was responsible for the exceptional beauty of the city of Florence. ∎

"Madonna della Seggiola" by Raphael

Ph. Bénet, R. Holzbachova/MICHELIN

■ Scoppio del Carro

This event – the Exploding of the Cart – is held in Piazza del Duomo. It dates from 1101, the year in which a crusader returned from Jerusalem with three stones from Christ's tomb. In each year that followed on Easter Sunday the stones produced sparks that were used to re-light the lamps extinguished on Good Friday.

From the 16C onwards the sparks began to light larger and larger "lamps" until the event acquired its present form. A wooden cart (6m/20ft high), known as *Il Brindellone*, is drawn through the streets by four oxen with gilded horns and hooves; it is accompanied by a procession of people dressed in Renaissance costume. On arrival in the square in front of the cathedral, the cart is unhitched; from the high altar in the cathedral a dove "flies" along a wire to the cart and sets off a cascade of fireworks. Then a young child draws lots to determine the order of play for the semi-finals of the football (*calcio*).

■ Rificolona

This festival takes place on the evening of 7 September, the eve of the Feast of the Birth of the Virgin. The tradition probably dates from the days when peasants from outlying country and mountain districts used to travel to Florence for the festival, hoping to sell their produce at the fair

Santa Reparata and the Scoppio del Carro

Although the present cathedral was dedicated to Santa Maria del Fiore, the people of Florence retained a place in their hearts for Reparata, the patron saint of the earlier cathedral. According to legend, when she was beheaded in Palestine at the age of 12, a dove flew out of her body to heaven.

Some people claim that this story inspired the metal dove which flies out of the cathedral on Easter Day to set off the cartload of fireworks.

which was held at that time. The long distances travelled by some of these visitors meant they spent several days on the road and had to carry lanterns when it was dark. The Florentines may have been thinking of these old-fashioned lights when they created the first paper lanterns (*rificolone*), which were originally in the shape of dolls, recalling the peasants who came down from the mountains to take part in the festivities. The lights consisted of a candle shaded by the doll's skirt, carried high in the air on the top of a long pole. Later the shape of the lanterns changed and people began to hang them in the windows of their houses.

■ Calcio Storico Fiorentino

Calcio is the name given to a sort of football played in 16C costume – the first match is on the Feast of St John the Baptist (24 June) and the two others on the following days. The matches are played by teams from the four districts of the city and consist of two semi-finals and one final. The game has no precise rules and is a combination of association and rugby football and wrestling. It is descended from the ball games played by the Romans in *Florentia*. The tradition was perpetuated into the Middle Ages when the town council was obliged to impose restrictions on the unruly players and their fans who invaded the streets and squares, disturbing the other citizens well into the night.

The present game commemorates a match played on 17 February 1530 when the city, which was under siege by the Holy Roman Emperor, Charles V, dared to demonstrate its defiance despite its privations, celebrating Carnival with much noise and clamour. Charles V was eventually victorious but the match went down in history.

The event begins with a huge procession of 530 players dressed in period costume. To the sound of trumpets and drums and with standards flying in the wind, the procession sets off from Santa Maria Novella to the square in front of Santa Croce, which is covered with sand for the occasion of the match. The kick-off is given by a blast on a culverin, which is also sounded each time a goal is scored. ■

From the Duomo to the Signoria

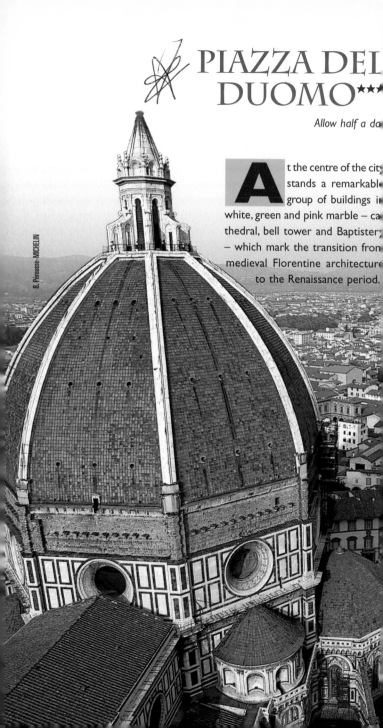

PIAZZA DEL DUOMO★★★

Allow half a da

A t the centre of the city stands a remarkabl group of buildings i white, green and pink marble – ca thedral, bell tower and Baptister – which mark the transition from medieval Florentine architecture to the Renaissance period.

B. Pérousse–MICHELIN

On the south side of the Piazza in the corner of Via dei Calzaiuoli stands the **Loggia del Bigallo**, which was built in the mid-14C with two perpendicular semicircular arcades surmounted by double windows. Lost or abandoned children used to be displayed beneath the loggia.

Duomo★★★

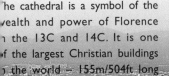

The cathedral is a symbol of the wealth and power of Florence in the 13C and 14C. It is one of the largest Christian buildings in the world – 155m/504ft long (St Peter's in Rome 186m/605ft long, St Paul's in London 152m/494ft long, Notre-Dame in Paris 130m/423ft long); 90m/293ft wide from one end of the transept to the other; 107m/348ft high from the floor to the top of the lantern. Its dedication to Santa Maria del Fiore recalls the flower, a golden rose, presented by Pope Eugenius IV when the cathedral was consecrated.

The cathedral was built on the site of the Romanesque cathedral of Santa Reparata, which was deemed too modest a building for

such an important city as medieval Florence. Its construction mobilised the resources of the city for almost 150 years.

The commission was given to the renowned architect, Arnolfo di Cambio, and, although work began in 1296, the cathedral was not consecrated until 1436. During this time considerable modifications to the initial plans were made by Arnolfo's successors, Giotto, Andrea Pisano and particularly Francesco Talenti.

The building, which is mainly Gothic, is a striking example of the original character of this particular style in Florence – large volumes and horizontal lines in preference to carved surfaces. A marquetry design of multi-coloured marble in typical Florentine style forms the geometrical decoration of the stone courses. The west front designed by Arnolfo di Cambio was demolished in 1588 without even being completed. It was replaced in the late 19C by the existing front, a complex imitation of the Gothic style.

The huge **dome*****, an integral part of the Florentine landscape is the most beautiful part of the building. It is the work of Filippo Brunelleschi, described by Vasari as "an architectural genius sent down by heaven to bring new form to an architecture that had gone astray"; in 1420 he solved the problem of how to roof the vast sanctuary. In order to reduce the massive thrust towards the centre of the dome, Brunelleschi designed a roof made of two flattened domes linked by a complex network of arches and buttresses. The construction of the gigantic dome, erected without any apparent support, aroused enormous admiration

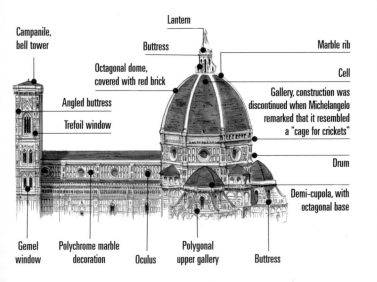

Lantern

Campanile, bell tower

Buttress

Marble rib

Octagonal dome, covered with red brick

Cell

Angled buttress

Gallery, construction was discontinued when Michelangelo remarked that it resembled a "cage for crickets"

Trefoil window

Drum

Demi-cupola, with octagonal base

Gemel window

Polychrome marble decoration

Oculus

Polygonal upper gallery

Buttress

and enthusiasm in Florence at the time. For almost 15 years the building site, with its hoists designed by Brunelleschi himself and capable of moving blocks of stone weighing over three tonnes, was an unprecedented sight for the Florentine people.

Exterior – *Starting on the south side, walk round the cathedral anticlockwise.* From the south side there is a striking view of the building; the amazing marble marquetry cladding accentuates the already grandiose appearance created by the lack of relief and the regular repetition of the various elements. The **east end★★★** is remarkably extensive consisting of three polygonal apses radiating from the transept crossing; together with the dome, which rests on a high drum, it forms a complex yet superbly well-balanced composition. Originally a gallery was to run round the base of the dome but its construction was apparently discontinued when Michelangelo remarked that it resembled a "cage for crickets".

On the north side of the building is the Mandorla Door, surmounted by a mandorla containing a carving of the *Virgin Mary of the Assumption* by Nanni di Banco in the early 15C. The mosaic work on the tympanum (1490) depicting the *Annunciation* is the work of Domenico Ghirlandaio.

Interior – After the lavish ornamentation of the exterior the nave is surprisingly plain. The small difference in height between nave and aisles, the four widely-spaced arches in the nave (80m/260ft long) and a cornice at the base of the vaulting break the verticality of the nave and seem to reduce the overall proportions of the building.

The stained-glass windows of the west end especially the central rose window depicting the *Assumption of the Virgin Mary*, were based on drawings by Lorenzo Ghiberti their composition uses a remarkable shade of green. The tomb of Bishop Antonio d'Orso who died in 1321, was carved by the Sienese sculptor, Tino di Ca-

Brunelleschi's dome, an integral part of the Florentine skyline

maino, who produced a number of famous monumental tombs during the Gothic period. A fragment of the original work *(left of the centre door)* shows the deceased asleep and seated, above a sarcophagus.

In the first bay of the south aisle, just above the place where his tomb was discovered in the crypt *(see below)* in 1972, is a portrait of Brunelleschi *(first medallion on the right on entering)* carved by one of his pupils.

In the north aisle are two frescoes containing equestrian sculptures in honour of two military men *(condottieri)* who hired their services to Florence; the first one is of Nicolò da Tolentino by Andrea del Castagno (1456) and the second one is of Giovanni Acuto by Paolo Uccello (1436). Another fresco, painted by Domenico Michelino in 1465, depicts Dante explaining his *Divine Comedy* to the city of Florence, which is represented by its cathedral as it was in the 15C; the fresco illustrates the "geography" of the other world as imagined by the poet – the pit of Hell, the mountain of Purgatory and the heavenly ranks of Paradise.

The aisles are lit by remarkable 14C stained-glass windows.

Sanctuary★★ – It is here that the true grandeur of the building can best be appreciated. The huge octagonal sanctuary is enclosed by an elegant marble screen erected in the mid-16C; from it radiate three vast apses forming a trefoil, each one containing five chapels. Above rises the breathtaking **dome★★★** (50m/162ft in diameter at its base and 91m/296ft high), which is decorated with a huge fresco depicting *The Last Judgement*; it was begun by Vasari who worked on it for two years from 1572 to 1574 but it required a further five years' work by Federico Zuccari before it was finished in 1579. Over the high altar hangs a wooden crucifix by Benedetto da Maiano (late 15C).

The tympanum above the door on the right leading to the Old Sacristy *(Sacrestia Vecchia)* is decorated with a terracotta *Ascension* by Luca della Robbia.

Beneath the altar in the axial chapel lies the tomb of St Zanobi, the first Bishop of Florence. This remarkable work consists of bronze reliefs depicting scenes

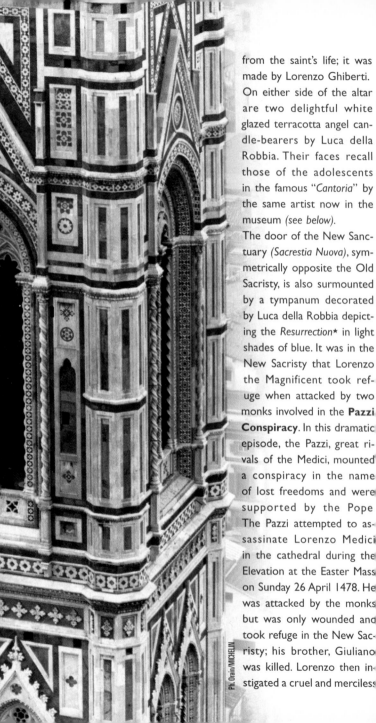

from the saint's life; it was made by Lorenzo Ghiberti. On either side of the altar are two delightful white glazed terracotta angel candle-bearers by Luca della Robbia. Their faces recall those of the adolescents in the famous "*Cantoria*" by the same artist now in the museum *(see below)*.

The door of the New Sanctuary *(Sacrestia Nuova)*, symmetrically opposite the Old Sacristy, is also surmounted by a tympanum decorated by Luca della Robbia depicting the *Resurrection*★ in light shades of blue. It was in the New Sacristy that Lorenzo the Magnificent took refuge when attacked by two monks involved in the **Pazzi Conspiracy**. In this dramatic episode, the Pazzi, great rivals of the Medici, mounted a conspiracy in the name of lost freedoms and were supported by the Pope. The Pazzi attempted to assassinate Lorenzo Medici in the cathedral during the Elevation at the Easter Mass on Sunday 26 April 1478. He was attacked by the monks but was only wounded and took refuge in the New Sacristy; his brother, Giuliano was killed. Lorenzo then instigated a cruel and merciless repression against the Pazzi. Skilful lighting shows off the **marquetry cabinets★** which were produced in the second half of the 15C, mainly by Benedetto and Giuliano da Maiano. The splendid bronze door panels depicting figures of the Evangelists and Prophets are also worthy of note.

Dome★★ – *Access via the north aisle. 463 steps.* The narrow gallery overlooking the chancel provides a breathtaking **view★★** down into the cathedral and also a close-up view of the remarkable **stained-glass windows★** in the oculi of the drum; they were produced in the first half of the 15C and are based on sketches made by the leading figures of the time – Ghiberti, Donatello, Paolo Uccello and Andrea del Sarto.

From the staircase leading to the top of the dome, which is constructed between the two vaults, there is an interesting view of the structural features; the final section, which is very steep and close against the wall, is the most spectacular. It leads to the exterior at the foot of the lantern turret which was Brunelleschi's last work and not set in place until after his death. From here there is a magnificent **panoramic view★★** of Florence – *(NW)* the dome of San Lorenzo backed by Santa Maria Novella standing out against the green of Cascine Park; *(left of the bell tower)* the arch of Piazza della Repubblica and cube-shaped Orsanmichele church,

backed *(south bank)* by the huge and impressive Pitti Palace and *(left)* the Boboli Gardens laid out on the hill. In the foreground *(S)* is the Loggia della Signoria and the Palazzo Vecchio in front of the long building of the Uffizi, flanked *(left)* by the slender bell tower of the Badia standing out against the massive outline of the Bargello. The light speck in the background is San Miniato near Piazzale Michelangolo. Slightly nearer *(SE)* is the white marble façade of Santa Croce. In the far distance *(N)* rises Fiesole Hill.

Santa Reparata's Crypt – *Staircase by the first pillar on the south side of the nave.* The crypt is in fact all that remains of an earlier Romanesque church (13C-14C), which was discovered during excavation work in 1966. It had itself been created through the conversion of a palaeo-Christian basilica (5C-6C) and was demolished during the construction of the present cathedral.

The place where Brunelleschi's tomb was discovered can be seen through an iron grille in an opening overlooking the uncovered section to the left of the staircase.

■ Campanile★★★

The straight lines of the slim, slender bell tower (82m/267ft high) form a harmonious contrast with the curved structure of Brunelleschi's dome.

The plans were the work of Giotto. Construction began in 1334, but he died in 1337. This gothic style tower, finished off at the end of the 14C, is quite unusual in its horizontal lines and geometrical ornamentation. Copies have replaced the original low reliefs in the bottom section of the building. The decoration was based on an overall design by Giotto. The first register was carved by Andrea Pisano and Luca della Robbia; the second by pupils of Andrea Pisano. The originals are in the Museo dell'Opera del Duomo.

From the upper terrace there is a fine **panoramic view**** of the cathedral and the city of Florence.

■ Battistero***

The baptistery, clad in white and dark-coloured marble, is a Romanesque style building, both sober and harmonious. The **bronze doors***** are famous throughout the world. The South Door *(now the entrance)* by Andrea Pisano (1330), distinctly Gothic in style, depicts scenes from the life of St John

the Baptist *(upper panel)*, and the Theological (Hope, Faith, Charity) and Cardinal Virtues. The Renaissance border, skilfully decorated, was the work of Vittorio Ghiberti, the son of the artist who produced the other two sets of doors. The North Door (1403-24) was the first work by Lorenzo Ghiberti, aged only 25, who won a competition in which the city's greatest artists, including Brunelleschi, Donatello and Jacopo della Quercia, took part. Scenes from the Life and Passion of Christ *(from bottom to top)* are depicted with remarkable austerity, nobility and harmony of composition. Facing the cathedral, the East Door (1425-1452) is the one which Michelangelo thought worthy to be called the Gate of Paradise. Ghiberti illustrated episodes from the Old Testament, with figures of the Prophets and Sibyls in the niches. The artist has depicted himself as a bald and roguish-looking man, set in a medallion.

Ph. Orain/MICHELIN

Ph. Orain/MICHELIN

Interior – It is imposing and majestic (25m/82ft in diameter), with its black and white marble-clad walls and its pavement adorned with eastern motifs. The dome is covered in sparkling 13C **mosaics*****. The large Christ in Majesty is flanked on both sides by the Last Judgement; on the five concentric registers covering the other five sections of the dome are depicted *(from top to bottom)*: Celestial hierarchies, Genesis, The Life of Joseph, The Life of the Virgin Mary and Jesus, The Life of St John the Baptist.

To the right of the apse is the tomb of the Antipope John XXIII (c.1370-1419), Cosimo the Elder. It is a remarkable work produced in 1427 by Donatello assisted by Michelozzo.

■ Museo dell'Opera del Duomo**

The museum houses artefacts from the cathedral, the bell-tower and the baptistery. On the mezzanine floor is the famous *Pietà*** sculpted by Michelangelo. The great hall *(first floor)* houses *Mary Magdalen** repenting, the prophets Jeremiah and Habakkuk (nicknamed *Zuccone* (marrow) because of the shape of his bald head), the famous **Cantorie**** (choir galleries) in the cathedral by Luca della Robbia and Donatello. The museum also contains the magnificent **silver altar**** depicting the story of John the Baptist (14C-15C) and the admirable **low reliefs****, some of which depict various trades and activities as well as scenes from the Book of Genesis, produced by Andrea Pisano and Luca della Robbia. ■

Ph. Orain/MICHELIN

PIAZZA DELLA SIGNORIA★★

This was the political centre of Florence. Set against the backcloth of the Palazzo Vecchio, the Loggia della Signoria and, in the wings, the Palazzo degli Uffizi, the vast piazza is decorated with numerous statues which make it a veritable open-air museum. In the middle of the square is an equestrian statue of Cosimo I by Giovanni da Bologna; at the corner of the Palazzo Vecchio is the Neptune Fountain (1576) by Bartolomeo Ammannati. Copies of the *Marzocco,* (the lion of Florence) by Donatello and of *David*, by Michelangelo have been placed in front of the Palazzo itself.

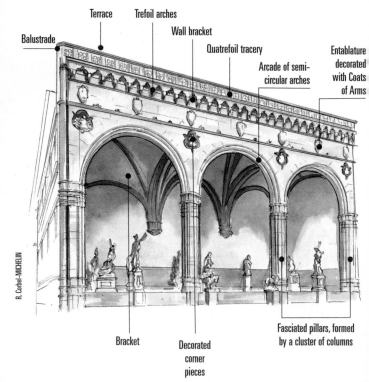

Terrace

Trefoil arches

Wall bracket

Balustrade

Quatrefoil tracery

Entablature decorated with Coats of Arms

Arcade of semi-circular arches

Fasciated pillars, formed by a cluster of columns

Bracket

Decorated corner pieces

R. Corbel–MICHELIN

■ Loggia della Signoria★★

Built at the end of the 14C, it first housed the city's government, then was used as a guard room by the *Lanzi*, Cosimo I's lancers. Statues dating from the days of the Ancient Romans *(restored)* and the Renaissance have been placed in the loggia: the *Rape of the Sabine Women* (1583) and *Hercules Slaying the Centaur, Nessus* by Giovanni da Bologna. Also note the admirable statue of **Perseus**★★★ brandishing the head of the Medusa, made between 1545 and 1553 by Benvenuto Cellini.

Ph. Orain/MICHELIN

■ Palazzo Vecchio or Palazzo della Signoria***

The impressive mass of the palazzo, surmounted by an elegant tower, dominates the square. It was built between 1299 and 1314, and probably designed by Arnolfo di Cambio. It is in an austere Gothic style, characterised by the absence of windows on the lower level; a series of twin windows on the first floor, and machicolations, parapet walkways and crenellations where the tower stands.

The luxurious, elegant Renaissance interior forms a striking contrast to the exterior. The **courtyard***, totally redesigned in the 15C by Michelozzo, was elegantly decorated a century later by Vasari. In the centre is a graceful fountain surmounted by a small winged genius (16C), a copy of a bronze by Verrocchio (the original is inside the building).

The building was designed to house the city government (la Signoria). In the 16C Cosimo I made the building his residence and also adapted it to suit the grand-ducal court. When Cosimo I left the building and moved to the Pitti Palace, it became known as Palazzo Vecchio (Old Palace) instead of Palazzo della Signoria. The rooms were magnificently decorated with sculptures by Benedetto and Giuliano Maiano (15C) and paintings by Vasari and Bronzino (16C) in praise of the city of Florence and the Medici family.

On the first floor, the Hall of the Five Hundred (Salone dei Cinquecento), painted by several artists including Vasari, contains a sculptural group by Michelangelo depicting Genius slaying Might. The walls of the sumptuous **Studiolo**** (study) of Francesco de Medici, designed by Vasari, were painted by Florentine Mannerist painters like Bronzino, the author of the portraits of Cosimo I and Eleonora of Toledo. Vasari and his pupils decorated Leo X's apartments with scenes depicting the life of the Medici family.

The second floor contains three suites of rooms (quartieri) – the Priors' Apartment, note the **Lily Chamber*** (Sala dei Gigli) with its superb coffered ceiling by Giuliano da Maiano and the **Map Chamber*** (Sala delle Carte Geografiche) whose walls are covered with 16C maps; Eleonora of Toledo's Apartments, decorated by Vasari, except for the chapel ornate with frescoes by Bronzino; and Cosimo I's Apartment, known as "the Elements Apartments", named after the allegorical scenes in the decoration of the first room. ∎

MUSEUMS

GALLERIA DEGLI UFFIZI★★★

Allow 2hr 30min.

This is one of the finest art museums in the world. These collections were assembled by several generations of Medici and the visitor can follow the evolution of Italian art from its beginnings to the 17C. The early nucleus was gathered together by Francesco I (1541-87) to which were added the collections of the Grand Dukes Ferdinand I and II, and Cosimo III. In 1737 the last member of the Medici dynasty, Anna Maria Luisa, Electress Palatine, bequeathed the Medici collection to her native city of Florence. The Uffizi Museum was then housed in the Renaissance palace, designed by Vasari in 1560, which contained the offices *(uffizi)* of the Medici administration.

The rich collections of drawings and paintings are on the first floor; paintings and sculptures are exhibited in 45 rooms which are linked by two galleries on the second floor.

The first gallery is dedicated to Florentine and Tuscan artists: there are works by Cimabue, Giotto, Duccio, Simone Martini (the *Annunciation*), Paolo Uccello *(Battle of San Romano)* and Filippo Lippi.

The Battle of San Romano

Room 7 (early Renaissance – 15C) is dominated by Paolo Uccello's famous *Battle of San Romano*, one panel of a huge triptych. The other sections are in the Louvre Museum in Paris and the National Gallery in London. The painter laid the battle out like a geometrical composition and structured the space with a view to achieving a sense of perspective, one of the main concerns of Renaissance artists. By making daring use of foreshortening and reducing certain features (soldiers) to mere volume through the unusual use of colour (red horses), he set himself apart from his contemporaries and gave his work a modern, abstract character which has often led him to be considered as a distant precursor of Cubism.

The **Botticelli Room★★★** is the gallery's crowning glory. Apart from a series of world-famous pictures by the Renaissance master, it also contains splendid works indicating the reciprocal influence of Florentine painters and Flemish Primitives that accompanied the commercial exchanges of the 15C. Botticelli's major works *(from left to right)* include the *Madonna of the Magnificat*, a roundel including remarkable intricacy of detail and extraordinary harmony. From the peak of the artist's career comes the allegorical *Birth of Venus* and *(next wall) Primavera*, undoubtedly the most representative examples of Botticelli's poetic lyricism and the idealism that characterised the Humanist culture favoured at the court of Lorenzo the Magnificent. In the *Birth of Venus*, a young woman expressing a melancholy and fragile

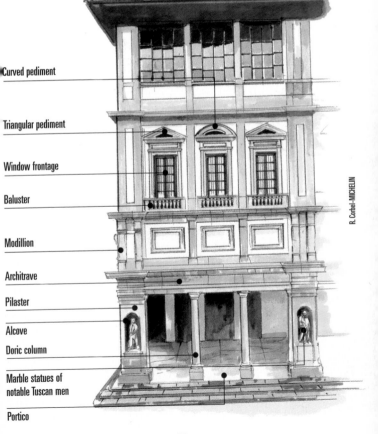

Curved pediment

Triangular pediment

Window frontage

Baluster

Modillion

Architrave

Pilaster

Alcove

Doric column

Marble statues of notable Tuscan men

Portico

R. Corbel-MICHELIN

grace emerges from a background of sea and sky painted in remarkably transparent cold tones; the artist is said to have represented the features of Simonetta Vespucci, mistress of Giuliano, the brother of Lorenzo the Magnificent. The undulating outlines of the fabrics, the loose flowing hair and the slightly bent figure of Venus give the scene a graceful dance-like quality.

Other exhibits in the gallery include the *Adoration of the Magi* and the *Annunciation* by Leonardo da Vinci and a series of Italian and foreign paintings from the 15C and 16C (Perugino, Cranach, Dürer, Bellini, Giorgione, Correggio).

Room 25 provides an introduction to the High Renaissance (16C) through work by Michelangelo and the Florentine School. The famous **Tondo Doni** painted by Michelangelo in 1503, depicts the Holy Family against a background of young nudes. The artist's talents as a sculptor are obvious in the powerful rendering of his figures, while the perfection of the glaze where not one brushstroke is visible is evidence of mastery acquired only by painters. The complexity of the composition, in which the Virgin Mary seems to be frozen in such a position that it is impossible to tell whether she is taking the child from Joseph or offering the infant to him, expresses

Botticelli's "Primavera" takes mythology to new heights of purity and harmony

Piazza della Signoria

PALAZZO VECCHIO

Terrace

Via   della   Ninna

Bar

Chiasso dei Baroncelli

45

44

43

Corridor

Piazzale

degli

Uffizi

Corridor

3   4

2   5-6

7

8   9

N

Sala
di
Niobe
42

★★★ Sala del
Botticelli
10-14

41

15   16

17

Rotunda

18
Tribune

35

19

Corridoio
del Cinquecento

20

21

31   34

32   33

22

29

23

28   27   26

24

30

25

GALLERIA DEGLI UFFIZI
First floor

0   20 m

Corridor

Lungarno Luisa de' Medici

⬍   Lift

     Highly recommended rooms

The Primavera

The scene takes place in Venus' garden. The goddess is in the centre of the composition, surrounded by orange trees and myrtle bushes. Above her flies Cupid, his arrow aimed at one of the three Graces, who are dancing with each other and are unaware of his presence. To the left, Mercury disperses the clouds with his caduceus, while to the right the green-coloured Zephyr pursues the nymph Cloris. Ovid recounts that after marrying the nymph Zephyr made her queen of the flowers. Thus transformed, Flora scatters roses over the flower-decked meadow.

There have been many interpretations of this work, which could be seen as a portrayal of the metamorphosis of love. The shy and dreamy young woman about to be hit by the arrow could be *Castitas*, the girl to the left, *Voluptas*, and the third figure, *Pulchritudo*. *Castitas*, at whom Cupid is aiming, seems to be moving towards *Voluptas*, while *Pulchritudo* maintains the balance of the three figures. Venus is a static figure, presiding in the centre over these games of love.

Mercury, who was thought to accompany souls to the next world, acted as a messenger between men and the gods; here he reaches up to the sky, watched by *Castitas* who is inspired by a higher love. The harmony of the painting lies in its balanced composition: Mercury's upward motion is balanced by the figure of Zephyr at the opposite side of the painting, who stretches down towards the ground.

Michelangelo's own tormented character. The contortion of the bodies paves the way for Mannerism and can be seen again in later works, especially in many of the figures within the Sistine Chapel. **Room 28** contains 16C Venetian paintings and displays a number of works by Titian including the *Venus of Urbino (right-hand wall)*, one of the artist's late masterpieces (1538). The intimacy of the scene, the languid attitude of the character and the dazzling nude placed obliquely across the painting and contrasting with the sombre tones of the background, show a sensuality and warmth far

removed from the severity that characterised Florentine art at this time.

Room 43 is dedicated to Caravaggio (1573-1610). The artist was only 20 when he painted the famous *Adolescent Bacchus*, a bright, vivid oil painting as yet devoid of the brutal contrasts of light and shade that were to characterise most of his work. The young god depicted as a popular character is a clear indication of the naturalistic style which was to have such considerable impact on 17C-18C European art.

▮ Corridoio Vasariano

This gallery (1km/0.5mi long), which conveys a sense of secrecy and adventure, was commissioned by Cosimo I so that he could pass unseen and apart from the crowds from the Palazzo Vecchio to the Pitti Palace. It was built by Vasari in only five months in 1565 and runs from the Uffizi, through the top storey of the buildings on the Ponte Vecchio, before penetrating the maze of houses on the south bank of the Arno. The charm and beauty of this unusual location is enhanced by the view through the windows of Florence, the Arno and the surrounding hills. The corridor forms a coda to the Uffizi galleries and is hung with 17C and 18C works and famous self-portraits.

The first paintings are from the school of Caravaggio (*Adoration of the Christ child* by Gherardo delle Notti), followed by works from other Italian schools – Bologna (Guido Reni, Albani, Guercino), Venice (Liss), Rome (Bamboccio), Tuscany (Lorenzo Lippi) and Naples (Salvator Rosa). The 17C Lombardy artists are represented by Giovanni Battista Crespi, and 18C Venetians by Bellotto and Rosalba Carriera. The French school is represented by La Tour, La Hyre and Boucher.

The section of the corridor above the Ponte Vecchio is lined by about a hundred self-portraits by Titian, Veronese, Rosalba Carriera and Correggio. The remaining section of the corridor is hung with portraits by Velázquez, Rubens, Élisabeth Vigée-Lebrun, Ingres, Delacroix and Chagall; it provides a view of the interior of the church of **Santa Felicità**, rebuilt in the 18C, and ends at the Pitti Palace. ▮

GALLERIA DELL'ACCADEMIA★★

Allow 30 min

The Accademia is of exceptional interest for its collection of sculptures by Michelangelo. The gallery also houses an art collection of mainly Florentine works dating from the 13C-19C.

The first room contains paintings from the late 15C and early 16C, including a fine *Deposition* by Filippino Lippi and Perugino *(opposite the entrance)*; it has an almost Mannerist quality in the flowing lines formed by the strips of cloth used

to bring Christ down from the cross. The plaster cast group in the middle of the room is the model produced by Giovanni da Bologna for his *Rape of the Sabine Women* in the Loggia della Signoria.

■ **Michelangelo Gallery★★★**
On either side of the gallery are four of the famous *Slaves* (the other two are in the Louvre Museum in Paris), allegories for the soul imprisoned in the body, made for the tomb of Pope Julius II in Rome. A

A Hero For the Florentine Republic

The biblical hero who defeated the giant Goliath, symbolised the determination of the Florentine Republic to defend its freedom in the face of its enemies, however powerful they might be. In contrast to older works, David is nervously poised for action with sling in hand, not yet experiencing the serenity and pride of victory. He stands with his body weight on his right leg to suggest – using the "contrapposto" technique – the tension arising immediately before movement. The artist also broke with tradition by portraying the character, not as a frail adolescent, but rather as a muscular young man whose consummate beauty makes him reminiscent of an Apollo from Antiquity.

umber of designs were produced or this mausoleum which was originally intended to include 40 huge statues and to be erected in the centre of St Peter's in Rome; the final version is in the Church of St Peter in Chains in Rome. In their contorted movements, the unfinished figures (1513-20) seem to be attempting to break free from the marble from which they emerge; they convey a feeling of strength and pathos.

Flanked by the two Slaves *(right)* is St Matthew, part of a series of 12 statues of the Apostles that Michelangelo was commissioned to produce for the cathedral; this statue too is only roughly carved and the others were never produced.

The so-called *Palestrina Pietà*, together with the Pietà in the Museo dell'Opera del Duomo and the *Rondanini Pietà* in Milan, represents the final apotheosis of Michelangelo's art. The overdeveloped arms and torso and roughly carved legs, portrayed with unusual foreshortening, suggest the heaviness of Christ's dead body and illustrate the artist's remarkable knowledge of human anatomy.

At the end of the room stands the huge statue of *David*, in an apse that was specially built for the work in 1873. Michelangelo was 25 years old and already immensely famous when he carved this masterpiece (1501-04), one of his most famous sculptures, from an enormous block of marble that was considered to be unusable.

The statue was placed in front of the Palazzo Vecchio where it remained until 1873.

■ Pinacoteca★

In the Art Gallery, the first of the three small adjoining rooms *(right of the main gallery)* displays the front panel of the famous Adimari Chest *(second bay on the right)* depicting the wedding celebrations held in Florence for one of the members of this aristocratic family. The artist, an unknown 15C painter referred to as the "Master of the Adimari Chest", has captured in a fresh, lively style, one moment in the life of some of his wealthiest contemporaries, depicting in detail the costumes, headresses and ceremonial artefacts of the time. In the background are the Baptistery and surrounding houses. ■

PALAZZO DEL PODESTÀ E MUSEO NAZIONALE DEL BARGELLO★★★

Allow 1hr 30min

This forbidding **palaz-zo★** is a fine example of medieval vernacular architecture. The oldest part of the façade, surmounted by an el-egant tower with merlons, was buil in the mid-13C. It originally housec the Capitano del Popolo, who rep-resented the working classes within the Florentine government, then the

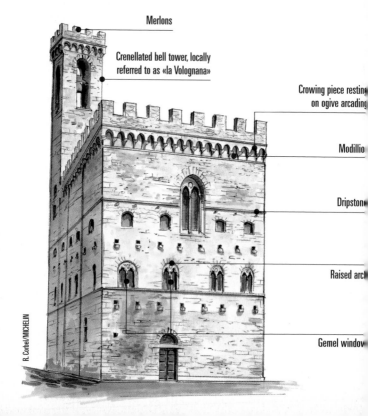

Merlons

Crenellated bell tower, locally referred to as «la Volognana»

Crowing piece restin on ogive arcadin

Modillio

Dripston

Raised arc

Gemel window

R. Corbel/MICHELIN

The David

The famous bronze *David* is a masterpiece dating from Donatello's more mature period. The adolescent, crowned with a laurel wreath, is a symbol of hope overcoming brute strength. Standing with legs slightly apart, he strikes a pose of detached pride. The splendid body, tensed yet carved in gentle relief, is the expression of an artistry that had reached the height of perfection.

Podestà, the first magistrate who held executive and judicial powers. The later part of the building, which is lower and less austere in appearance, was built in the Gothic style a century later. In 1574 the building became the residence of the Chief of Police (called Bargello) and part of it was turned into a prison.

The severity of the **courtyard★★** is softened by a porch with wide arcades and a loggia reached by a picturesque outside staircase.

In fact, this is one of the finest medieval courtyards in Italy. The coats of arms of the magistrates *(podeste)* who lived in the palace from the 14C to 16C provide a charming decoration. Condemned prisoners were put to death beside the well.

The ground floor contains 16C works by Michelangelo (*Tondo Pitti, Brutus, Drunken Bacchus*) and by Benvenuto Cellini (low-reliefs of his *Perseus*).

Cortile del Bargello (detail)

Ph. Orain/MICHELIN

Beneath the vaulting there is an outstanding **collection of works★★★** by **Donatello**, whose genius dominated the Early Italian Renaissance. There is a small lively bronze *Cupid*. The marble statue of *David* is one of the artist's early work (1409) showing a realistic observation far removed from the Gothic tradition and the more famous bronze *David*. The famous *"Marzocco"*, the Florence lion, whose paw rests on the city's shield

Ph. Drain/MICHELIN

stood for many years in front of the Palazzo Vecchio.

The imposing *St George (in the niche in the end wall)* originally stood outside Orsanmichele; it is an early work (1416) which still displays a certain Gothic stiffness.

The Verrocchio Room contains a collection of several sculptures by the Florentine artist who, as both painter and sculptor, was one of the leading figures of the Italian Renaissance. Near the centre of the room stands the famous bronze *David*, dating from c 1465 and sculpted for the young Lorenzo the Magnificent and his brother, Giuliano, whom Verrocchio had befriended. Like Donatello's works, whose themes Verrocchio used repeatedly, the biblical hero is depicted as a delicate yet determined adolescent, and is treated with grace and sensitivity. ■

The palazzo's façade and the inner court (left) share an austere elegance

CONVENTO
E MUSEO DI
S. MARCO★★

The museum in a former Dominican monastery, rebuilt c 1436 in a very plain style by Michelozzo, contains **works★★★** by **Fra Angelico**. Fra Angelico took orders in Fiesole before coming to St Mark's, where he decorated the walls of the monks' cells with edifying scenes. Humility, gentleness and mysticism were the qualities expressed by this artistic monk in a technique influenced by the Gothic tradition. His refined use of colour, delicate draughtsmanship and gentle handling of the subject matter imbued these frescoes with a pacifying power, particularly appropriate for this oasis of calm and place of meditation.

The former guest hall, opening off the cloisters on the right, contain many of the artist's works on wood, especially the triptych depicting the *Descent from the Cross,* the famou *Last Judgement* and other religiou scenes. The chapter house has a se vere *Crucifixion* while the refector contains an admirable *Last Supper* by Ghirlandaio.

The staircase leading to the firs floor is dominated by Fra An gelico's well-balanced and sobe masterpiece, the *Annunciation★★★* The monks' cells open off thre corridors, with lovely timber ceilings. Along the corridor to the lef of the stairs are the *Apparition o Christ to the Penitent Magdalen (1st cell on the left),* the *Transfiguration (6th cell on the left)* and the *Coronation of the Virgin (9th cell o the left).* At the far end of the next corridor are the cells of Savonarola, who was prior of St Mark's Off the corridor on the right is the **library★**, one of Michelozzo's finest achievements. ■

Fra Angelico

Fra Giovanni da Fiesole, better known by the name of Fra Angelico, was born in the latter years of the 14C in Vicchio, 30km/19mi northeast of Florence. He entered the Dominican Order in Fiesole and later came to St Mark's in Florence where he spent about ten years covering the walls of the cells and conventual rooms with edifying scenes designed to inspire meditation.

Through his art this modest monk achieved fame within his own lifetime. He was called to Rome on several occasions by Pope Eugenius IV and Pope Nicholas V; the latter commissioned him to decorate the Papal chapel in the Vatican. Orvieto Cathedral has some admirable frescoes painted by him. He also produced numerous altarpieces.

He died in 1455 during a visit to Rome and for several centuries bore the title "Blessed" *(Beato)* until he was eventually canonised in 1983.

His paintings are characterised by their serenity, tenderness and humility. Although he was deeply attached to the Gothic tradition and therefore often worked on triptychs, creating golden backgrounds and using the precious style of the miniaturist, he was also attracted by the new Renaissance theories, as is shown by a certain number of his works in which the figures are steeped in a sense of humanity and space is structured in such a way as to hint at perspective. His altar paintings and frescoes, which are true acts of faith, are impressive for the simple mysticism of his vision and the purity of line and colour. In many cases he worked with his pupil, Benozzo Gozzoli, and with Filippo Lippi, and it is sometimes difficult to distinguish what was actually painted by him.

OTHER MUSEUMS

■ Museo Archeologico★★

The museum has an important collection of Egyptian, Greek (*François vase*★★, found in an Etruscan tomb but of ancient origin), Etruscan (*Arezzo Chimera*★★, a 5C BC masterpiece) and Roman art.

■ Opificio delle Pietre Dure★

The **Hard Stone Workshop** upholds one of the grand traditions of Florentine craftwork. The chief decorative motifs are flowers, fruits and birds.

■ Museo della Fondazione Horne★

Horne (1864-1916) was a British collector who devoted his life to restoring this small palace. Among the works of art and furniture which contribute to the beauty of the mansion, note the low relief depicting the *Madonna with Child*, by Sansovino, the *San Stefano* by Giotto, and the paintings by Dosso Dossi, Signorelli, Masaccio, Lorenzetti, Gozzoli, Beccafumi, Filippino Lippi, Simone Martini.

■ Museo della Casa Fiorentina Antica★

The **Old Florentine House Museum** is housed on the three floors of the **Palazzo Davanzati★**, a narrow, towering residence built in the 14C for a rich wool merchant and purchased in the 16C by the historian and man of letters, Bernardo Davanzati. It was at this time that the typical loggia at the top of the building was added beneath the overhanging roof. The building was superbly restored at the turn of the century and it contains a splendid collection of furniture (mainly Florentine or Tuscan from the 14C, 15C and 16C).

■ Museo Marino Marini★

Sculptures, paintings, drawings and engravings show the artist's marked interest in the austere, static plastic art of ancient statuary onto which he grafted an anxiety typical of his day. The main themes represented are Woman, the Horseman and the Warrior.

■ Museo La Specola★

This natural history museum which was founded in 1775 by Grand Duke Leopold, is named after the astronomical and meteorological observatory (*specola* in Italian) which was installed at the request of the Grand Duke. It houses an extensive zoological collection and over 600 amazingly lifelike anatomical waxworks (*Rooms XXV-XXXIII*).

Museo Stibbert⋆

The Stibbert Villa (19C) stands at the entrance to a small park filled with trees. It now houses the huge art collections built up during the last century by Federico Stibbert, the Anglo-Italian Garibaldian hero – arms and armour, sculptures, paintings, furniture, faïence, tapestries, embroidery, objects and costumes of varying origins and periods of history (Renaissance to the 19C). Special mention must be made of the hundreds of pieces of **old armour⋆⋆**.

Museo Bardini⋆

The collections of this museum all bequeathed to the city in 1922 by Stefano Bardini, a famous antique dealer, are indicative of his eclectic taste: sculptures, stucco work, paintings, small bronzes and medals, Persian rugs (16C-17C), tapestries made in the 18C in Florence workshops, ceramics and old musical instruments.

Museo di Storia della Scienza⋆

The Museum of the History of Science is housed in the austere medieval **Palazzo Castellani**. It displays a vast collection of ancient scientific instruments. Many of the exhibits come from the collections built up by the Medici family and the Grand Dukes of Lorraine. The fourth room is one of the most important because it contains memorabilia relating to Galileo.

Museo Storico Topografico "Firenze Com'era"

In the Museum of Topographical History of Florence, paintings, engravings and old maps trace urban development in Florence from the Renaissance to the 19C.

Casa Buonarroti⋆

It consists of a group of houses purchased in March 1508 by Michelangelo at the corner of Via Ghibellina and the alleyway at right angles to it. It is thought that he lived in one of them. The building contains a large collection of memorabilia relating to the family and also the collections built up by his great-nephew who was most interested in art and most devoted to the great master. ■

Palazzo Davanzati

R. Corbel-MICHELIN

FLORENCE UNDER LORENZO DE' MEDICI

SAN LORENZO★★★

St Lawrence's Church★★ is situated close to the Medici Palace *(now the Palazzo Medici-Riccardi),* and was formerly the Medici family parish church (several members of the Medici family bore the name Lorenzo). For over three centuries it was also their burial place. Construction of the church was begun c 1420 by Brunelleschi, who was commissioned to undertake the work by Giovanni di Bicci, Cosimo the Elder's father. Subsequent generations of the Medici family added their own embellishments.

As in the case of a number of other Florentine churches, the harsh façade never received the marble cladding included in the designs. The huge dome that caps the rear of the building is part of the Princes' Chapel, which was added in the 17C.

For the interior Brunelleschi broke with Gothic conventions and introduced a style that became typical of the Florentine Renaissance. He adopted the traditional basilica layout – nave and two aisles – of the former building with 11C restorations, and combined its Romanesque structures – semicircular arches, for which Florence retained a certain preference – with features taken from ancient Greek and Roman architecture – Corinthian columns, fluted pilasters, cornices.

The interior is a perfect example of the sobriety of style

introduced by Brunelleschi and typical of his thoughtful, measured, rigorous architectural style and its human dimension. His great achievement is the **Old Sacristy★★** *(at the far end of the north transept).* Donatello was responsible for part of the decoration of this and also the two **pulpits★★** in the nave with bronze panels, which are works of admirable virtuosity and full of a great sense of drama.

■ Biblioteca Medicea Laurenziana★★

Cosimo the Elder's library was added to by Lorenzo the Magnificent. Access is from the north aisle of the church or through the charming 15C **cloisters★** *(entrance to the left of the church).*

Vestibolo – To decorate this exceptionally small yet disproportionately tall vestibule, the artist divided the walls into sections in an unusual way using architectural features that are normally found only on façades, while at the same time playing on the contrast between the

white surfaces and grey *pietra serena* relief. The unusual use of huge twin columns, heavy cornices on brackets and window frames set flat against the wall already heralds the Baroque era. This style is further emphasised by the volutes on the consoles and the splendid monumental three-flight **staircase****, in which the width of the treads increases towards the bottom, creating an impression of a waterfall. Michelangelo left for Rome in 1534, where he settled permanently, and the staircase was left at the planning stage. It was completed in 1559 by the Mannerist architect, Ammannati, who used the original drawings and acted in accordance with the numerous instructions sent to him by Michelangelo from Rome.

Sala di lettura – Although the architectural style is more austere, the Reading Room has its own charm because of the strict geometrical lines that are systematically repeated along the whole length of the room, creating a remarkable sense of perspective. The desks and lavish coffered ceiling, carved in wood were both designed by Michelangelo. The fine terracotta flooring from the same period is by Tribolo (the designer of the Boboli gardens).

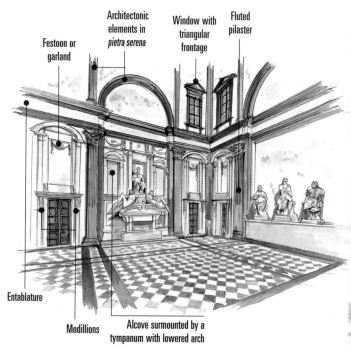

Festoon or garland

Architectonic elements in *pietra serena*

Window with triangular frontage

Fluted pilaster

Entablature

Modillions

Alcove surmounted by a tympanum with lowered arch

Cappelle Medicee★★

Entrance on Piazza Madonna degli Aldobrandini. The term Medici Chapels is used to refer the Princes' Chapel and the New Sacristy.

The Princes' Chapel (17C-18C), grandiose but gloomy, is faced with semi-precious stones and marbles and is the funerary chapel for Cosimo I and his descendants.

The New Sacristy was Michelangelo's first architectural work and despite its name was always intended as a funerary chapel. Begun in 1520, it was left unfinished when the artist left Florence in 1534.

Michelangelo achieved a great sense of rhythm and solemnity by using contrasting materials, dark grey sandstone *(pietra serena)* and the white of the walls and marbles. The famous **Medici tombs★★★** were also the work of Michelangelo.

The monumental group was to be composed of four mausoleums but only two were in fact completed. On the right is the tomb of Giuliano, Duke of Nemours (son of Lorenzo the Magnificent), who died in 1516 at the age of 35; Giuliano is portrayed as a Roman Emperor holding the baton of an army commander on his knees.

At his feet are the famous semi-reclining allegorical figures of *Day* (unfinished), conveying a powerful energy, and *Night*, sleeping in a pose of graceful abandon. Opposite is the tomb of Lorenzo, Duke of Urbino (the grandson of Lorenzo the Magnificent and father of Caterina de' Medici), who died in 1519 at the age of 27; he is shown in meditation and at his feet lie the other two famous statues depicting *Dusk*, in the guise of a melancholy old man, and *Dawn*, portrayed as a woman rising uneasily from her slumber. Each of these marble figures conveys a tragic grandeur and remarkable vigour. It is possible that the two idealised figures were intended to represent *Action* and *Thought* triumphing over Time which, through the different stages of life (symbolised by times of the day), leads man to his death. The only work to be produced for the tomb of Lorenzo the Magnificent *(right of the entrance)* is the admirable *Madonna and Child,* a work showing a remarkably sharp sense of observation and understanding. Lorenzo, the most famous of the Medici, lies with his brother Giuliano in the plain sarcophagus below. ■

PALAZZO
MEDICI-RICCARDI★★

Allow 30 mi

This noble but austere building is typical of the Florentine Renaissance with its mathematical plan and rustication, massive at ground level and lighter on the upper level. The palace which has a square arcaded courtyard was begun in 1444 by Michelozzo on the orders of his friend Cosimo the Elder. From 1459 to 1540 it was a Medici residence, and Lorenzo the Magnificent held court here, attended by poets, philosophers and artists alike.

■ Cappella★★★

First floor: entrance by the first stair way on the right in the courtyar This tiny chapel was decorate with admirable frescoes (1459) b **Benozzo Gozzoli**. *The Processio of the Magi* is a vivid picture o Florentine life with portraits o the Medici and of famous digni taries from the east who ha assembled for the Counci of Florence in 1439.

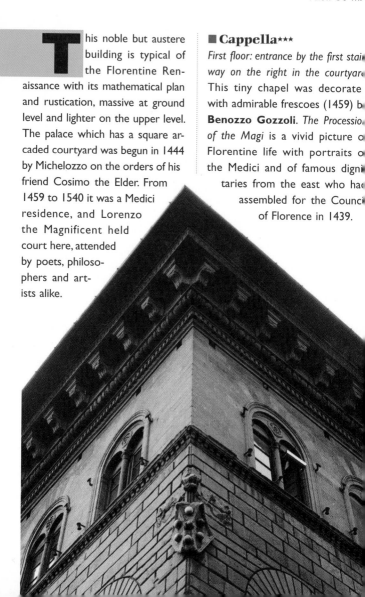

A Closer Look at the Procession of the Magi

There are those who have claimed that the young horseman in blue with the cheetah *(left-hand wall)* in front of the Three Kings, is Giuliano, Lorenzo's brother. The Three Kings, representing the three ages of life, are portrayals of other major figures of contemporary society. At the head of the procession *(left-hand corner)* is the patriarch of Constantinople who died in Florence during the Council. Behind him, dressed in a splendid green and gold coat and Oriental headress, is the Byzantine Emperor John VIII Palaeologus, riding a magnificently harnessed horse *(wall opposite the altar – right of the entrance)*. At the end *(right-hand wall)*, clothed in a beige and gold jerkin and mounted on a palfrey (the harness bears the Medici coat of arms), is the young Lorenzo the Magnificent. Behind him on the white horse is his father Piero I. In the middle of the group behind him is a self-portrait of Benozzo; his cap bears the inscription "Opus Benotii". The three adolescent girls on horseback *(left-hand corner of the wall opposite the altar)*, who are dressed in light-coloured tunics, are Giuliano and Lorenzo's sisters.

▮ Sala di Luca Giordano★★

First floor: entrance by the second stairway on the right in the courtyard. The entire roof of this gallery built by the Riccardi at the end of the 17C and splendidly decorated with gold stucco, carved panels and great painted mirrors, is covered by a brightly-coloured Baroque fresco of the *Apotheosis of the second Medici dynasty*, masterfully painted by Luca Giordano in 1683. ■

On the South Bank of the Arno

PONTE VECCHIO ★

The Old Bridge is the oldest bridge in Florence, built at the narrowest point on the course of the Arno, near where a Roman bridge once spanned the river carrying the road linking Rome to northern Italy. Over the centuries the bridge was destroyed on a number of occasions; the current structure dates only from 1345. In 1944 it was the only bridge in Florence to be spared by the Germans who, in order to block the advance of American troops approaching from the south, razed the surrounding old districts almost entirely t the ground (one medieval towe standing on the north bank slight upstream of the entrance to th bridge survived). The Ponte Vec chio did, however, suffer extensiv damage during the 1966 floods. The arcades that initially lined th bridge housed the tanners' work shops and, later, the stalls of butch ers for whom the river provided handy "sewer". In the 16C, on th orders of Grand Duke Ferdinand the butchers were forced to mak way for craftsmen whose activitie were of a less insanitary and mor

decorative nature – jewellers and gold and silversmiths who built most of the tiny corbelled shops above the Arno still occupied by craftsmen today. The shops attract a continuous flow of visitors, who come to buy or just to look and who throng the bridge during the summer season until late in the evening.

The esplanade in the middle of the bridge contains a bronze bust of the most famous goldsmith of all, Benvenuto Cellini, placed there in the 19C. From here, there is a fine view of the banks of the Arno and the succession of bridges that span it.

Walk towards the Palazzo Pitti, passing in front of the Church of **Santa Felicita**. Above the entrance porch is a sumptuous chamber, resembling a box at the theatre, where the Grand Dukes could attend Mass. The chapel *(immediately to the right of the entrance)*, built in the early 15C by Brunelleschi, contains the famous *Deposition*★★ by **Pontormo**, painted in clear sharp tones with undulating, elongated forms in a style characteristic of Tuscan Mannerism. ■

PALAZZO PITTI ★★

Allow Half a day

The Pitti Palace is a huge Renaissance palace built round three sides of a sloping square overlooked by the building's long, severe façade. Only the shading of the heavy rustication work softens the imposing architectural style and breaks up a unity verging on the monotonous.

Work began on the palace in 1458. It was designed for the Pitti, a family of influential merchants and bankers who were initially friends but later great rivals of the Medici. The building then consisted of no more than the section comprising the seven central bays. Several years later the Pitti family was financially ruined and the residence designed to outshine their rivals was left unfinished.

The palace was bought in 1549 by Eleonora of Toledo, wife of Cosimo I, and she turned it into a princely residence to which Cosimo I transferred his court c 1560. The work of conversion was entrusted to the architect and sculptor, Ammannati. The hillside was laid out as a magnificent garden but it was not until the 17C that the front of the building

attained its current length (over 200m/650ft). The two projecting wings were added in the 18C.

■ Galleria Palatina★★★

The Palatine Gallery takes its name from the title of the last of the Medici, Anna Maria Ludovica (1667-1743), who was married to the Elector Palatine. The luxurious interior houses an outstanding collection of 16C, 17C and 18C works, including a series of **paintings★★★** by Raphael (*Portrait of a Lady* or *La Velata, Madonna del Granduca* and *Madonna della Seggiola*) and Titian (portraits of *La Bella, The Aretino, The Concert* and the *Grey-eyed Nobleman*), which make the Pitti Palace one of the richest art galleries in the world.

■ Appartamenti Reali★

Access via the foyer of the Palatine Gallery. First Floor. The Royal Apartments extending from the centre of the façade to the end of the right wing had always been used as state rooms or private apartments by Tuscany's three ruling families – the Medici, the Grand Dukes of Lorraine and the House of Savoy sovereigns of Italy when Florence became the capital city (1865-70)

Ph. Orain/MICHELIN

■ Galleria d'Arte Moderna★

bove the Palatine Gallery. The Gallery of Modern Art is housed in neo-Classical setting created for he Grand Dukes of Lorraine by he architect Poccianti. The exhibition is of mainly Tuscan work **works★★ by the Macchiaioli**), lustrating the various trends that nspired Italian painting and sculpure from the late 18C to the early ecades of the 20C.

■ Museo degli Argenti★★

Ground floor and mezzanine. The entrance is situated at the far left of the Ammannati courtyard. The outstanding collections of the Silver Museum consist mainly of the treasures of the Medici family and House of Lorraine. Most of the exhibits were made in the workshops of Florence but others were added to the grand ducal treasure after being brought from Germany or Austria, first on the occasion

"Madonna della Seggiola" by Raphael

Ph. Bénet, R. Holzbachova/MICHELIN

of the marriage of Anna Maria Ludovica to the Elector Palatine following the union of the houses of Lorraine and Habsburg, and secondly during the Napoleonic occupation after the period spent in exile in Austria by Ferdinand II of Lorraine.

■ **Galleria del Costume**★ *Meridian Pavilion. Access by lift situated in the ticket office and staircase leading to the Palatine Gallery.* The Costume Gallery offers an insight into the history of fashion from the 18C to c 1930 through its extensive collection of costumes, shoes, linen and accessories. There is a reconstruction of the burial clothes of Eleonora of Toledo and her husband, Cosimo I, based on the remnants found in their tomb. ■

A Closer Look at the Paintings

In the portrait of the famous *Veiled Lady (La Velata)* Raphael displays his skill as a brilliant colourist using a range of shades based almost exclusively on browns, golds and whites. The flowing outlines, the solid harmony created by the opulent forms and abundance of rounded contours, and the sheer extravagance of the shimmering iridescent fabric, make this work a masterpiece. The model may have been the famous Fornarina, the artist's beloved.

The Madonna of the Grand Duke, of which Grand Duke Ferdinand III of Lorraine was so enamoured that he refused to be separated from it, was painted c 1505 in Florence. At that time Raphael was influenced by both Michelangelo and Leonardo, borrowing from the latter the technique of vague contours better known as *sfumato*. The shining pale golden shades of the Virgin Mary's serene, tender face, and the gentleness which exudes from the painting are reminiscent of Perugino, who was Raphael's teacher.

The *Madonna della Seggiola* was painted a few years later and the artist, at the peak of his talent, uses a more subtle and varied palette. The gentle serenity of the faces, graceful positions and mysticism so characteristic of religious scenes, is combined with a force generated by the forms and pictorial structure (emphasised by the round composition that suggests circular movement, a reminder of Michelangelo's influence).

GIARDINO DI BOBOLI⋆

The Boboli Gardens were begun in 1549 when Cosimo I commissioned the architect, sculptor and landscape gardener, Nicolo Pericoli alias Tribolo, to convert the hill behind the Pitti Palace into a vast garden; together with Ammannati's courtyard and the terrace, it was to be the setting for the lavish pageants held by the Grand Dukes. When Tribolo died the following year, he had only drawn up the plans. He was succeeded in 1550 by Ammannati then in 1583 by Buontalenti, who both added a number of refinements to the original design.

The entrance is situated on the far side of the inner courtyard. A flight of steps leads to the terrace which is separated from the rear of the palace by the elegant Artichoke Fountain (Carciofo), built in 1641.

The 17C amphitheatre, where extravagant entertainments were once held, dominates the centre of the park. In 1841 the Royal House of Lorraine had a Roman granite basin and a 2C BC Egyptian obelisk from Thebes placed in the centre. Walk towards the top of the hill before reaching the first terrace turn right into an uphill path which leads to a circle. This part of the gardens, covering the hillside, was not laid out until the early 17C. The long and steep **Viottolone**⋆ (opposite) descends majestically between a double row of age-old pines and cypress trees to the charming circular **Piazzale dell'Isolotto**⋆; at the centre is a round lake adorned with statues; in the middle of the lake is an

The Ocean Fountain in the Boboli Gardens

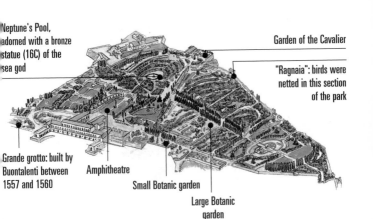

Neptune's Pool, adorned with a bronze statue (16C) of the sea god

Garden of the Cavalier

"Ragnaia": birds were netted in this section of the park

Grande grotto: built by Buontalenti between 1557 and 1560

Amphitheatre

Small Botanic garden

Large Botanic garden

island with orange and lemon trees and the Ocean Fountain, carved by Giovanni da Bologna in 1576. The standing figure represents Neptune; the three others symbolise rivers.

On turning back towards the palace, visitors see Neptune's Pool, adorned with a bronze statue (16C) of the sea god and, on the following terrace, a statue of Plenty which was begun by Giovanni da Bologna and finished in 1636 by the Florentine, Pietro Tacca.

A short path (right) leads to the Porcelain Museum.

The path *(left)* leads to the foot of the Belvedere Fort *(access now restricted by a gate)*. Further down stands the Kaffeehaus, an extravagant and predominantly red edifice built by Zanobi del Rosse in 1776 and evidence of the 18C taste for exoticism. From the bar patio, there is a **fine view★** of Florence. *Walk back down towards the palace and turn right into the wide ramp.*

At the end is a path leading to the Grotta grande, a fanciful creation designed mainly by Buontalenti (1587-97) and consisting of several chambers decorated with basins, statues, paintings, stalactites and a form of Rococo decoration depicting sheep, goats, shepherds, etc. The walls were once the backdrop to a multitude of waterfalls. The small Bacchus Fountain *(right near the exit)* includes a monstrous figure, one of Cosimo I's midgets, astride a tortoise.

■ Museo delle Porcellane★ (Porcelain Museum)

A double-flight staircase leads to the delightful Cavaliere Pavilion which was built for Cosimo III in the late 17C. In front of the building is a small terraced garden overlooking the exquisite Florentine countryside. The building houses a rich collection of Sèvres, Augarten and Meissen porcelain. ■

CHIESA DI
SANTO SPIRITO*

This Renaissance church designed by Brunelleschi is situated at the end of a peaceful, shady square off the main tourist track.

The modest façade covered with light rendering and the south side with its three tiers of structural features do not figure in Brunelleschi's plans, but are nevertheless fairly harmonious constructions.

The solemnity of the interior forms a stark contrast with the simplicity of the exterior and is in many respects reminiscent of the church of San Lorenzo – same contrasting colours created by the use of *pietra serena* emphasising the architectural lines against the light rendering, same full semicircular arches, same

purity of lines, same geometrical ordering of space. In this church however, the arcades separating the nave from the aisles extend in an unbroken line around the transept and flat chevet, accentuating the effect of unity and creating numerous perspectives. Supporting the arches are magnificent monolithic columns with Corinthian capitals surmounted by a high entablature. The building includes 38 small semicircular chapels which, according to Brunelleschi's plans, were doubtless intended to be visible from the outside. The chapels open into the aisles through arches of the same height as those in the nave and it is this that gives the church its remarkably spacious character.

Michelangelo's Crucifix

In 1492, Michelangelo sculpted a wooden crucifix and gave it to the church of Santo Spirito in recognition of the services of the church's prior, who had helped him with his dissections in his study of anatomy. According to the art historian Vasari, with this wooden crucifix, Michelangelo gave a hint of his future genius. At the time, the Crucifix was located above the master altar; after its restoration, it was placed in the sacristy.

Santo Spirito contains numerous **works of art*** – a delightful painting by Filippino Lippi *(fifth chapel in the south transept)* depicting, against a picturesque landscape background, a *Madonna and Child (second chapel in the south transept)* a *Virgin surrounded by Saints* by Lorenzo di Credi *(first chapel in the apse)*, a polyptych by Maso di Banco (an early 14C Florentine painter, who studied under Giotto) portraying the *Madonna and Child between four saints; (second chapel in the apse)*, an elegant painting by Alessandro Allori depicting *Christ and the Adulteress (second chapel in the apse)* and the Corbinelli Chapel *(at the far end of the north transept)*

containing an ornate carved marble reredos dating from the early 16C by Andrea Sansovino.

The splendid **sacristy*** *(entrance in north aisle by the door next to the second chapel)* is a monumental construction designed in 1489 by Giuliano da Sangallo in the spirit of Brunelleschi's designs. It is preceded by an impressive columned vestibule roofed with a deep barrel vault with carved panelling that was completed in 1495 by Cronaca, the architect of the Palazzo Strozzi.

Cenacolo di Santo Spirito – *Left of the church – n° 29.* The fine Gothic hall with bare rafters is the former refectory of the Augustinian friary adjoining the church. One of its walls is covered by a large *Crucifixion*, a fresco painted c 1360, and the remains of the *Last Supper (above)*, which are attributed to Andrea Orcagna and Nardo di Cione. The refectory also displays sculptures dating from the Romanesque to the Baroque periods. ∎

SANTA MARIA DEL CARMINE: FRESCOES IN THE BRANCACCI CHAPEL ★★★

What makes this church, which was ravaged by fire in the 18C, so interesting is the extraordinary series of frescoes decorating the walls of the Brancacci Chapel at the end of the south transept, one of the few parts of the building to have escaped fire damage. They were painted by three different artists and describe original sin and the life of St Peter; the latter subject was probably chosen because Florence had political links with the Papacy.

■ Affreschi di Masolino da Panicale (Frescoes)

Masolino was the first artist to be commissioned, in 1424, to undertake the decoration of the chapel built for the Brancacci, a family of silk merchants. Although the spirit of his work is still noticeably Gothic, as is obvious from his kindly, serene treatment of the subject matter, there is already an attempt to render perspective and volume. He was probably influenced in this respect by his pupil, Masaccio. On the upper section, he depicted the *Temptation of Adam and Eve*, *St Peter raising Tabitha from the Dead*, and *St Peter Preaching*.

■ Affreschi di Masaccio (Frescoes)

This chapel is a fine example of the innovatory genius of this artist, who pointed the way forward to the Renaissance through his feeling for relief and expression. In 1427, when he was no more than 25 years old, shortly before his death in 1428, he created this set of frescoes that are now considered as one of the most consummate examples of Italian painting in existence.

In his famous painting of *Adam and Eve being expelled from Paradise*, symmetrically opposite the *Temptation* painted by Masolino, he totally excluded idealism in order to express, with poignant intensity, the shame and despair of the figures. The light projected onto the scene and the splashes of shadow that conceal certain parts of the bodies and faces add to the dramatic effect and accentuate the impression of relief, giving the figures a striking reality.

The Tribute Money depicts the Apostles as vigorous figures radiating supreme gravity. The fresco includes three episodes, reduced to their main elements. They show the tax-collector (rear view) at the Capernaum Gate, demanding payment of the toll from Jesus who is showing Peter the water in which he will find the fish with the silver coin in its mouth (central scene). The Apostle takes hold of the fish (left), then hands the coin over to the tax-collector (right).

Another fresco depicts St Peter baptising and St Peter curing the lame man. This scene was painted with Masolino whose regular, more anecdotal style is obvious in the two elegant figures crossing the square.

■ Affreschi di Filippino Lippi (Frescoes)

The decoration of the chapel was still incomplete by the time Masaccio left for Rome. It was completed in 1481 by Filippino Lippi who painted the following scenes in an elegant style (on the lower section of the wall): St Paul visiting St Peter in prison in Antioch; St Peter raising the Son of Theophilus, Prefect of Antioch, from the dead, a fresco which had been started by Masaccio; St Peter set free by an Angel during his second term of imprisonment in Jerusalem and St Peter and St Paul arguing with Simon Magus before the Emperor and the Crucifixion of St Peter.

The two faces beside the altar piece are portraits of Masaccio and Masolino. ■

Masaccio (1401-28) and the Introduction of Volume in Painting

Masaccio died prematurely at the age of 27 after travelling to Rome with Donatello and Brunelleschi. He was to painting what his two friends were to sculpture and architecture. From the former, he acquired a taste for powerful figures, realistic expressions and heavy draped clothing; from the latter, he learned about perspective which he then applied not only to illustrations of buildings but also to human figures as in his frescoes in Santa Maria Novella. He discovered that light contained sculptural resources and concentrated on giving volume to his figures and improving his spatial layout, leaving aside the grace, ornamentation and excessive detail of the Gothic style. He paved the way for the Renaissance style in painting and his works had a huge impact on successive generations because of their lifelike realism.

RELIGIOUS AND ARTISTIC SIGHTS

S. MARIA NOVELLA**

The church and cloisters of Santa Maria Novella stand at the north end of the irregularly shaped Piazza Santa Maria Novella, which was laid out in the 14C; the south side is lined by the Renaissance arches of the long, slightly elevated Loggia de San Paolo. In the Middle Ages the square was used for numerous tournaments and other pageants and from the mid-16C to the last century it hosted the Palio dei Cocchi, the chariot race held on St John's Day (24 June), which was introduced by Cosimo I and based on the two-horse chariot (*biga*) races of Ancient Rome. The Grand Dukes presided over the event from a canopied box set up on the steps of the loggia.

The central area was divided into two tracks by a rope stretched between two wooden pyramids which were replaced in the 17C by marble obelisks designed by Giovanni da Bologna.

Although the Dominicans commenced work on the **Church of Santa Maria Novella**★★ in 1279 in an attempt to heal the rift between the Guelphs and Ghibellines, the main part of the building was not completed until 1360.

The lower part of the extremely elegant façade with its light geometrical design picked out in green and white marble, dates from the mid-14C. In 1458 the work was taken over by Leon Battista Alberti, who succeeded in blending

Restored Masterpieces

In spring 2001, after many years of restoration, the *Crucifixion* (1288-90) by **Giotto** and the *Trinità* (1424) by **Masaccio** are again on view.

The *Crucifixion*★ has been replaced in the nave where it used to be before Vasari reorganised the church in 1565. As a result of the restoration work, the original figure of Jesus in watercolours has been uncovered under the paint. The *Trinità* is in the north aisle. It is hard to believe that this fresco was completed in 27 days.

the existing Gothic features with the Renaissance style by creating an overall structure based on simple forms such as squares and circles. The central doorway, pillars and the whole of the upper section of the façade were built to his plans. The remarkable voluted consoles in coloured marble marquetry were designed to fill the space between the aisles and the higher nave. This treatment was then adopted in a great number of Renaissance churches and in Baroque façades. Funding for the work was provided by the Rucel-

lai, a rich family of merchants, whose dedicatory inscription – IOHANES.ORICELLARIVS.PAV .F.AN.SAL. MCCCLXX – adorns the pediment. The Rucellai coat of arms, a billowing sail, appears in the middle frieze.

Above the twin recesses at each end of the façade there is a sundial (*right*) and an armillary sphere (*left*).

The small cemetery (*right*), where Domenico Ghirlandaio was buried, is enclosed by a screen composed of a series of Gothic recesses which like those on the façade contain the remains of Florentine families. At the base of the recesses are marble sarcophagi carved with the People's Cross and the coats of arms of the families of the deceased.

B. Morandi/MICHELIN

From Piazza dell'Unità Italiana and Piazza della Stazione there is a remarkable **view*** of the powerful chevet, surmounted by a slender, austere Romanesque Gothic bell tower.

Inside, in the north aisle, the famous fresco of the *Trinity***, painted by Masaccio, is a work which is of vital importance in the history of Art. In this fresco he broke away from the attractive elegance of Gothic painting by painting God the Father in a Renaissance setting, holding the upright of the Cross and presenting the sacrifice of His crucified Son. The outline of the Holy Ghost in the form of a dove stands out on His chest. Christ is flanked by the Virgin Mary (her face and outstretched hand also show that she has accepted the sacrifice), St John and the donors, on their knees. An austere alternation of pink and blue shows the extent to which the artist emphasised the drawing rather than the colour. In this work Masaccio made use of new mathematical theories on perspective, drawn up by Brunelleschi, and so achieved one of the finest and earliest examples of architectural perspective. The faces of the figures, which are seen from below, show the determination for realism which is another of this artist's main characteristics.

At the far end of the north transept, the Strozzi di Mantora Chapel (raised) is decorated with **frescoes*** (1357) by the Florentine Nardo di Cione depicting the Last Judgement on a grand scale. The **polyptych*** on the altar is by Nardo's brother, Orcagna di Cione. The sacristy contains a fine *Crucifix** *(above the entrance)* by Giotto and a delicate glazed terracotta **niche*** by Giovanni della Robbia. In the Gondi Chapel *(first on the left of the high altar)* is displayed the famous *Crucifix*** by Brunelleschi, which so struck Donatello that he is said, on first seeing it, to have dropped the basket of eggs he was carrying. The chancel is ornamented with admirable **frescoes***** by **Domenico Ghirlandaio** who, on the theme

of the Lives of the Virgin and of St John the Baptist, painted a dazzling picture of Florentine life in the Renaissance era.

The church is flanked by two cloisters. The finest are the **Chiostro Verde★** (Green Cloisters), so called after the dominant colour of the frescoes painted by Paolo Uccello and his school (scenes from the Old Testament). Opening off these to the north is the **Cappellone degli Spagnoli★★** (Spaniards' Chapel) with late-14C **frescoes★★** by Andrea di Bonaiuto (also known as Andrea da Firenze). With an intricate symbolism the frescoes depict the Church Triumphant and the glorification of the deeds of the Dominicans. To the east is the refectory which houses the church's treasure. ■

Farmacia di Santa Maria Novella

The pharmacy of Sant Maria Novella was founded in 1221 when the Dominicans first came to Florence. It has also sold spices since the 16C and their scents waft out into the street. The large shop is set out in an old chapel with ogival vaulting which was dedicated to St Nicholas. It was built in 1332 and redecorated in the neo-Gothic style in 1848. The room which opens on to the cloisters, now a herbalist shop selling a range of fragrant herbs, has stucco-work vaulting and 17C furnishings including display cabinets containing numerous stills. The frescoes in **St Nicholas' Sacristy** depict *Christ's Passion*.

SANTA CROCE★★

Allow 1hr 30min

The white marble façade of the Church of the Holy Cross fills the east side of a vast square, Piazza Santa Croce, one of the oldest and most grandiose squares in the city.

This was one of the worst affected districts during the 1966 floods and Santa Croce was one of the historic buildings of Florence which suffered most from the mud that reached a height of three metres inside the church and up to five metres in the cloisters.

■ Church★★

This is the church of the Franciscans. It was started in 1294 and completed in the second half of the 14C. The façade and the campanile date from the 19C. The interior is vast (140m x 40m/460ft x 130ft) as the church was designed for preaching and consists of a single spacious nave and slender apse with fine 15C stained-glass windows. Because of the 276 gravestones set in the pavement and the lavish tombs contained in the church, Santa Croce has been nicknamed the "Italian Pantheon".

South Aisle: By the first pillar, a *Virgin and Child* by Antonio Rossellino (15C); opposite, the tomb of Michelangelo (d 1564) by Vasari opposite the second pillar, the funerary monument (19C) to Dante (d 1321, buried at Ravenna); by the third pillar, a fine **pulpit★** (1476) by Benedetto da Maiano and facing it the monument to V Alfieri (d 1803) by Canova; opposite the fourth pillar, the 18C monument to Machiavelli (d 1527); facing the fifth pillar, an elegant low relief of the *Annunciation★★* carved in stone and embellished with gold by Donatello; opposite the sixth pillar, the **tomb of Leonardo Bruni★★** (humanist and chancellor of the Republic, d 1444) by Bernardo Rossellino, and next to it the tomb of the composer Rossini (d 1868).

South Transept: At the far end, the Baroncelli Chapel with **frescoes★** (1338) depicting the Life of the Virgin by Taddeo Gaddi and at the altar, the **polyptych★** of the Coronation of the Virgin from Giotto's studio.

La Cappella dei Pazzi: a saf resting-place for the treasure of Santa Croce

Sacristy★ *(access by the corridor on the right of the chancel)*: This dates from the 14C and is adorned with **frescoes★** including a Crucifixion by Taddeo Gaddi and, in the fine Rinuccini Chapel, with scenes from the Life of the Virgin and of Mary Magdalene by Giovanni da Milano (14C).

At the far end of the corridor is the harmonious Medici Chapel (1434) built by Michelozzo, with a fine **altarpiece★** in glazed terracotta by Andrea della Robbia.

Chancel: The first chapel to the right of the altar contains evocative **frescoes★★** (c 1320) by Giotto depicting the life of St Francis; in the third chapel is the tomb of Julie Clary, the wife of Joseph Bonaparte. The chancel proper is covered with **frescoes★** (1380) by Agnolo Gaddi relating the legend of the Holy Cross.

North Transept: At the far end is a famous *Crucifixion★* by Donatello, which Brunelleschi tried to surpass at Santa Maria Novella.

North Aisle *(coming back)*: Beyond the second pillar, a fine monument to **Carlo Marsuppini★** by Desiderio da Settignano (15C); facing the fourth pillar the tombstone of L. Ghiberti (d 1455); the last tomb (18C) is that of Galileo (d 1642).

■ Cappella dei Pazzi★★

The Pazzi Chapel, one of the most exquisite of the designs generally attributed to Brunelleschi, was built for the Pazzis, who were the main rivals of the Medici. The artist worked on the chapel until 1445, the year before his death, but it was not completed until c 1460.

The portico is reminiscent of Classical triumphal arches because of its raised central arch, its Corinthian columns, and its entablature decorated with a frieze of medallions and divided off into sections with slim fluted pilasters. The central wooden

Ph. Orain/MICHELIN

door is by Benedetto da Maiano. The little cupola decorated with glazed terracotta and the medallion depicting St Andrew are the work of Luca della Robbia. Desiderio da Settignano designed the *putti* on the external entablature.

The interior is a masterpiece of Florentine Renaissance architecture. In this chapel Brunelleschi raised to perfection the architectural ideal that he had already expressed in the old sacristy in San Lorenzo. The layout is designed around a square with a ribbed central dome over pendentives. The rectangular apse is capped by a small circular dome. All the architectural features are emphasised by the grey of the *pietra serena* which stands out against the white pebble-dash in a manner that is strict yet elegant. A frieze of cherubim and mystic lambs, and glazed terracotta medallions by Luca della Robbia representing the Apostles *(on the walls)* and the Evangelists *(in the pendentives)*, probably by Brunelleschi, add a note of colour to the otherwise austere but harmonious interior.

A superb Renaissance doorway opens into the Great Cloisters. The vast and elegantly proportioned construction was designed by Brunelleschi shortly before his death and completed in 1453. Medallions, which were probably created by Bernardo Rossellino, decorate the squinches on the light arcades below a wide, open gallery including slender columns.

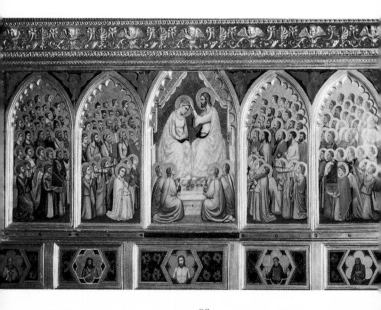

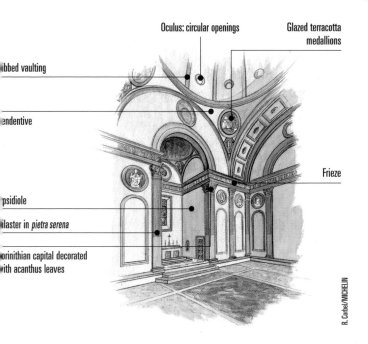

Oculus: circular openings

Glazed terracotta medallions

Ribbed vaulting

Pendentive

Frieze

Apsidiole

Pilaster in *pietra serena*

Corinithian capital decorated with acanthus leaves

R. Corbel/MICHELIN

Museo dell'Opera di Santa Croce
(Santa Croce Museum)

The old Franciscan chapter house, an elegant chamber with lancet windows and rafters, displays Cimabue's famous *Crucifixion*★, which has been restored with exemplary care after the considerable damage it suffered during the floods in 1966. Although large parts of the work have been lost, it still radiates an intense dramatic power through the way in which the body bends and sags.

The end wall is covered by a huge fresco representing the Last Supper; above is the Tree of the Cross, painted in the 14C by Taddeo Gaddi, to represent the genealogy of the Franciscans. ■

SANTA TRINITA

Holy Trinity Church was built in the second half of the 14C. The Baroque façade by Buontalenti was added in the late 16C.

The extremely austere, slender interior is a fine example of the beginnings of Gothic architecture in Florence. The façade of the Romanesque church built in the 11C can be seen incorporated into the current façade. It was revealed by restoration work carried out at the end of the last century.

The chapels contain some interesting works of art. The *Madonna in Majesty with Saints (third chapel in the south aisle)* is a 15C altarpiece by Neri di Bicci. The **Chapel of the Annunciation** *(fourth chapel)*, enclosed by a fine 15C screen and decorated with Lorenzo Monaco's frescoes recounting the Life of the Virgin Mary, contains a fine Gothic altarpiece by the same artist depicting the Annunciation; the predella in

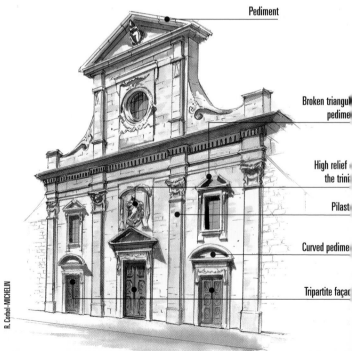

Pediment

Broken triangular pediment

High relief of the trinity

Pilaster

Curved pediment

Tripartite façade

R. Corbel-MICHELIN

ludes the Visitation, the Nativity, the Adoration of the Magi and the Flight into Egypt. The fifth chapel has an early 16C marble altar set in a splendid carved tempietto surround.

The main feature of interest in this church is, however, the decoration in the **Sassetti Chapel**** *(second chapel on the right in the south transept)* undertaken by Domenico Ghirlandaio in 1483. Using a technique he was later to employ in the chancel of Santa Maria Novella, the artist created a colourful portrait gallery of his contemporaries to depict episodes from the life of St Francis of Assisi – the *Renunciation of Worldly Goods (left-hand wall at the top)* and *(below) St Francis receiving the Stigmata* showing La Verna on the rock. The *Approval of the Franciscan Rule (end wall at the top)* shows in the background the Palazzo Vecchio and Loggia della Signoria, in the group standing *(right)* Lorenzo the Magnificent and the donor and his son *(left)* and in the immediate foreground emerging from the staircase, Poliziano with Lorenzo's three sons. The *Saint raising a child from the dead (below)* takes place in front of the Romanesque Santa Trinita Church. The *Trial by Fire before the Sultan (right-hand wall at the top)* is above the *Death of St Francis.* The vaulting is decorated with four splendid female figures representing Sibyls. The donors, Francesco Sassetti and his wife, are depicted kneeling. They both lie in the magnificent tombs with basalt sarcophagi – probably the work of Giuliano da Sangallo – on each side of the altar. Above is an *Adoration of the Shepherds,* another famous work by Domenico Ghirlandaio (1485). ■

OTHER PLACES OF WORSHIP

■ Orsanmichele★

Originally a grain storehouse, Orsanmichele was rebuilt in the 14C. There are works by Donatello, Ghiberti and Verrocchio. Inside, there is a splendid Gothic **tabernacle★★** by Orcagna.

■ La Badia

10C church. Note the **campanile★**. The interior has a sumptuous coffered **ceiling★★**, the **tombs★** and a delicate **lowrelief★★** sculpture in marble by Mino da Fiesole, and Filippino Lippi's *Virgin appearing to St Bernard★*.

The unusually shaped Orsanmichele church

Ph. Drain/MICHELIN

Sinagoga

The Florence Synagogue was built between 1874 and 1882 and was based on the Byzantine Agia Sophia in Constantinople. It is designed in the shape of a Greek cross surmounted by a bronze dome. The interior has a rich Moorish decoration including frescoes and mosaics, in addition to a superfluous pulpit in the Christian tradition. Part of the furniture originates from the two synagogues of the old ghetto which was located near Piazza della Repubblica. The Jews of Florence lived in a ghetto between 1571 (with authorisation from Cosimo I) and 1848, the year in which the restrictions were abolished. It was gradually demolished in the late 19C.

Chiostro dello Scalzo

The **Scalzo Cloisters**, small and intimate, contain a cycle of frescoes by Andrea del Sarto, painted in a warm shade of yellow ochre. Two of the 12 scenes depicting the life of St John the Baptist, the patron saint of the cloisters, were completed by Franciabigio.

Santissima Annunziata★

The Church of the Annunciation dates from the 15C. In the chancel are some fine **frescoes★** by Rosso Fiorentino and Pontormo which were completed by Franciabigio. The interior is in the Baroque style; the north arm of the transept gives access to the Renaissance Cloisters of the Dead (Chiostro dei Morti). The vault by

Light and shadow set off the clean lines of the Ospedale degli Innocenti

B. Juge-MICHELIN

One of the most beautiful squares in Florence and one of the Florentines' best-loved churches: Santissima Annunziata

the door is adorned with the *Madonna with the Sack*★ by Andrea del Sarto (16C).

■ Ospedale degli Innocenti★

Brunelleschi's **portico**★★ is decorated by terracotta **medallions**★★ by Andrea della Robbia. The Foundlings' Hospital houses a gallery displaying Florentine works.

■ Crocifissione del Perugino★

Perugino painted this fresco of the Crucifixion in the chapterhouse of the Benedictine convent of Santa Maria Maddalena dei Pazzi. The whole work is given a unity through the admirable Umbrian landscape portrayed with great depth and bathed in a gentle morning light. ■

CENACOLI
(OLD REFECTORIES)

■ Cenacolo di Ognissanti

The interior of the refectory of All Saints' Church contains two frescoes by Domenico Ghirlandaio and the tombstone by Amerigo Vespucci. On the north wall of the nave opposite is *St Jerome* by Ghirlandaio. Botticelli is buried in the south transept. The former refectory was decorated by Domenico Ghirlandaio in 1480 with a huge fresco of the *Last Supper*★, painted after the version in the Monastery of San Marco also by Ghirlandaio. These two works have numerous similarities, but the Last Supper in Ognissanti conveys a greater sense of serenity and is more natural owing to the slightly more austere decor and the very varied poses of the Apostles.

■ Cenacolo di Sant'Apollonia

The huge *Last Supper*★ covering one of the refectory walls is a masterpiece by Andrea del Castagno. It conveys great dramatic force because of the well structured framework, the relief achieved in the representation of the characters and the degree of realism.

■ Cenacolo di Fuligno

Its fresco of the *Last Supper*★ is attributed to Perugino. Jesus is about to speak, the gathering is serene. Judas is alone in the conventional manner, clutching his traitor's purse, and only Jesus and three Apostles are looking at him; John is still asleep. A certain theatrical effect is created by the splendid backdrop of a receding portico, in the centre of which the artist depicts Jesus praying on the Mount of Olives, suffused in soft lighting.

■ Cenacolo di San Salvi★

Andrea del Sarto painted the refectory's splendid *Last Supper*★★ inspired by the work of Leonardo da Vinci in Milan. It is an admirable example his restrained sensitivity and his taste for blending warm colours which he doubtless inherited from Raphael. The enclosed space, devoid of distracting details, is simply lit by an open air loggia where two characters watch the scene. The composition concentrates on the Apostles and Christ, who has just announced that one of the 12 will betray Him thereby provoking all possible reactions. The artist also broke with Florentine tradition by placing Judas to the right of Jesus, rather than setting him opposite, apart from the rest. ■

■ Palazzo Rucellai★★

The mansion was built between 1446 and 1451 by Bernardo Rossellino to plans by Leon Battista Alberti. The Rucellai were related created vertically by the alignment of pilasters and horizontally by the cornices that run along the top of each storey. The windows are set within these grid-like divisions

R. Corbel/MICHELIN

to the Strozzi and Medici. Their family emblem, a sail billowing in the wind, is depicted on a frieze on the first floor.

The mansion is the first example since Antiquity of a façade articulated by three orders superimposed. A rigorous sense of uniformity is against a background of slightly rusticated stonework which contrasts greatly with the heavy rustication on the ground floor of the Palazzo Medici and throughout the façade of the Palazzo Strozzi. Opposite stands the loggia attributed to Leon Battista Alberti.

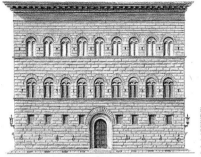

R. Corbel/MICHELIN

◼ Palazzo Strozzi★★

A rich merchant named Filippo Strozzi commissioned Benedetto da Maiano to design the building. In 1490, the year before he died, when building work had only just started, Filippo Strozzi commissioned Giuliano da Sangallo to produce a scale model of his future residence. It was, however, Simone di Pollaiolo, otherwise known as *Cronaca,* who eventually took charge of the work.

Cronaca is responsible for the splendid stone cornice at the very top of the building; its huge overhang and weight made it a feat of considerable technical prowess. Only part of the cornice, however, was completed, along the two sides of the building that overlook Piazza degli Strozzi and Via degli Strozzi. The building was finished in 1504 and remained in the Strozzi family until 1937. In contrast to the Palazzo Medici, where the typical rusticated stonework gives way to a gradually smoother surface on the upper storeys, here it covers the whole of the façade. The stately, elegant **courtyard**, surrounded by a high portico and overlooked by an open loggia on the upper floor, is the work of Cronaca. ◼

The sober harmony of the Florentine palazzi: Palazzo Rucellai (left) and Palazzo Strozzi (above)

OTHER PLACES OF INTEREST

■ Piazzale Michelangelo

From this vast esplanade overlooking the city, there is a magnificent **panoramic view★★★**. The memorial to Michelangelo, erected in 1875 in the centre of the square, is decorated with copies of some of the artist's most famous statues.

■ San Miniato al Monte★★

From Piazzale Michelangolo continue uphill away from the city along Via Galileo (part of Viale dei Colli); a steep flight of steps leads up to the church (left).

he church of San Miniato was
ilt in an outstandingly beautiful
tting** overlooking Florence,
the top of a wide flight of
eps commissioned by Poggi. It
flanked by a delightful graveyard
om which there is a view of the
untryside laid out like a picture
(left) the Boboli Gardens laid out
the hill below the Belvedere
rt which is distinguished by its
4C fortifications.

Benedictine monastery was
unded here in the 11C and its
urch is one of the finest exam-
es of Florentine Romanesque ar-
itecture. It was built in memory
f St Minias who fell victim to the
ersecutions ordered in AD 250
y the Roman Emperor Decius.

inias, probably a Tuscan of humble
rigins who, according to popular
elief, was a king from Armenia,
ad already miraculously escaped
number of executions. When
e had finally been beheaded, he
rossed the River Arno holding his
ead in his hands, returning to die
n the hillside where he had lived
s a hermit (then known as Mons
lorentinus).

s very elegant façade is decorated
with geometric designs in green
nd white marble, not unlike those

of the baptistery. The harmonious
interior also ornamented with
multicoloured marble contains
a 13C pavement. The **Chapel of
Cardinal James of Portugal***
opening out of the north aisle is
a fine Renaissance structure. In
the centre of the nave is a Chapel
of the Crucifix by Michelozzo.
The pulpit and chancel screen
(transenna) form a remarkable
ensemble** beautifully inlaid with
marble (early 13C). In the apse is a
mosaic depicting Christ giving His
Blessing. The **frescoes*** (1387) in
the sacristy are by Spinello Aretino.
The 11C crypt has delicate columns with Classical capitals.

■ Mercato Nuovo*

In the 16C Cosimo I ordered the
construction of this loggia with
elegant Renaissance arcades. Its
name, New Market Loggia, distinguished it from the old medieval
marketplace which once stood
nearby but was demolished in
the late 19C. Note the Porcellino
("piglet") Fountain, so named by
the people of Florence on account
of the bronze boar produced in
the early 17C by Pietro Tacca and
inspired by the Classical marble
sculpture exhibited in the Uffizi. ■

EXCURSIONS

■ From the Etruscans to the Florentines

Fiesole was founded by the Etruscans in the 7C or 6C BC and was the largest town in northern Etruria. The site had been chosen for its position on a rise commanding the routes which passed over the barrier of the Apennines *(north)* into the Arno Plain and continued south to Rome. This was, moreover, a healthier spot than the plain which in those days consisted largely of swamps. For several centuries Fiesole within its mighty walls was a town of greater power and importance than Florence.

Sulla set up a colony of Veterans here c 80 BC. In 63 BC the town rallied in support of Catiline who sought refuge here before the battle of Pistoia, where he was fatally wounded. From then on the destiny of Fiesole was linked to that of Rome. New buildings were erected on the ruins of the Etruscan structures and the Roman town, known as Faesulae, with its temples, theatre, and baths, became the main centre of the region. From the 1C AD onwards it began to fall into a decline and was overtaken by Florence, its rival and neighbour. In 1125 Faesulae was finally conquered by Florence and almost razed to the ground.

Fiesole is 8km/5mi NE of Florence. The two cities are linked by road S 65.
By bus: from Florence (Santa Maria Novella), line 7 of the ATAF company. The road winds uphill through olive-clad slopes, past luxuriant gardens and long lines of cypress trees. The route blends art and nature in a landscape reminiscent of a Renaissance style painting.

■ A City of Immutable Beauty

The arrival in Fiesole affords views of its incomparable **countryside★★★**.

The centre of Fiesole is the vast sloping square, which occupies the site of the old Roman Forum. On the north side stand an oratory Santa Maria Primerana with a late 16C portico, and the small 14 and 15C Palazzo Pretorio bearing the coats of arms of the magistrates *(podeste)* whose residence it used to be.

Opposite the cathedral entrance *(southwest corner)* a narrow and steep street, Via S Francesco, leads up to one of the heights, where the Acropolis of Faesulae stood in the Roman era. Half way up turn left into the small public park for fine **view★★** of Florence; the park projects like a balcony, overlooking the Arno Basin spread out below.

Basilica di Sant'Alessandro

The basilica (c 9C) was built on the site of a Roman temple which had been converted into a church by Theodoric (6C). The neo-Classical façade, added in 1815, is not inviting but the austere interior has a certain nobility; its nave and aisles are separated by superb Roman columns.

Convento di San Francesco★

This very modest friary, which is admirably located on the highest part of the hill, has been occupied by Franciscans since the early 15C. The tiny 14C cloisters *(entrance to the right of the church)* are visible through a wrought-iron grille. On the first floor *(steps to the left of*

the grille) are several of the tiny cells, furnished with plank bed, chest, desk and chair, where the friars used to live. One of them was occupied by St Bernardino of Siena who was Prior here for a few years.

The adjacent church, built in the mid-14C but with major alterations from subsequent periods, still has its original early 15C Gothic façade decorated with a small multifoiled canopy of simple design that is utterly charming. The church contains a number of interesting **paintings★**. On the south wall is an *Immaculate Conception* by Piero di Cosimo and, opposite it, an *Annunciation* by Raffaellino del Garbo.

The **Museo Missionario** (Franciscan Missions Museum – *access through the church*) contains a large collection of exhibits from the Orient (sculptures, paintings, clothing,

porcelain etc) and a small archaeology section (artefacts excavated near the friary, or Egyptian objects).

■ Duomo★

The cathedral is a Romanesque building, started in the 11C and extended in the 13C and 14C. Between 1878 and 1883, it was subjected to a massive restoration programme during which the façade was rebuilt. It is surmounted by a bell tower erected in 1213 which was altered in the 18C by the addition of merlons and machicolations to look like a belfry.

The stark **interior★** is laid out like a basilica with a chancel raised above the crypt, as in San Miniato in Florence.

Above the west door is a polychrome glazed terracotta niche by Giovanni della Robbia containing a statue of St Romulus, Bishop of Fiesole, to whom the cathedral was dedicated. The Salutati chapel *(right of the chancel)* is decorated with frescoes by Cosimo Rosselli (15C) and contains two delightful **works★** by Mino da Fiesole – the tomb of

Leonardo Salutati (including a bus of the Bishop) and a carved reredo representing the Virgin Mary wit the young St John and other saint

■ Zona Archeologica

In an enchanting **setting★** on a hill side clothed in cypress trees ar the remains of several Etrusca and Roman buildings. The archaeo logical items found on the site hav been placed in a small museum t the right of the entrance.

Excavations – The **Roman the atre★** *(teatro romano)* dates fron 80 BC. It was buried for several cen turies and was not excavated unt the end of the 18C. Its 23 tiers c seats are well preserved; the centra portion is set into the hillside an the first four rows were reserve for VIPs. At the foot of the tiers c seats is the semicircular orchestra once paved with multicoloure marble. Behind the orchestra, on slightly higher level, was the stage The front curved inwards in th centre and was decorated with frieze of carved marble reliefs, nov

in the museum. Behind the stage, in the base of the wall forming the backdrop, were the openings by which the actors made their entrances and exits.

To the left beyond the theatre was a small Etruscan temple *(tempietto etrusco)* built towards the end of the 4C BC. It was partly destroyed by fire; the remains were then integrated into a new building constructed during the days of Sulla. The rectangular layout of the building is still apparent, as are the steps leading up to it.

To the right are a few fragments of the Etruscan walls.

Opposite the temple and to the right of the theatre, were the baths *(terme)* built by the Romans in the 1C AD. Three arches have been reconstructed. The baths were composed of an open-air section, consisting of two large rectangular swimming pools, the second of which had two basins, and at the rear, under cover, the hot baths *(caldarium)* where the floor was supported on small brick pillars around which hot air circulated *(hypocaust)*.

Museo Archeologico★ – The Archaeological Museum is organised so that most of the exhibits are laid out according to their place of origin; thus objects from very different periods are presented together.

Room I contains the items found during the restoration of the town walls. In the second room are funeral items excavated from the graves in an Etruscan necropolis, which was used in later years by the Romans and lay beside one of the main roads leading into the town; displayed alone in a small glass case is a cylindrical lead **urn**★ *(cista)*, thought to date from the 3C or 4C AD, which contained burnt bones and ashes, when it was discovered, but would originally have been used to carry hot water for Roman baths or banquets; its final use may be attributable to its having become too worn for its original purpose.

The third room contains objects from the Archaeology Zone, among which are antefixes (sort of gargoyle) in the shape of female figures and tiny bronze votive offerings, some of which are shaped like feet or legs; they date from the period prior to Roman colonisation. Against the wall at the end of the room is a row of fragments of the carved marble frieze which once decorated the stage in the theatre (games in honour of Dionysius).

The rooms on the first floor house exhibits relating to the Later Roman Empire and the Middle Ages. The first room displays objects excavated in tombs found on the site of the main square and in the Archaeology Zone – bottles, iron belt ornaments dating from the 7C-8C (case 28), gold threads found on the arms and chest of a male burial (case 38), pearls from a necklace (case 39), and silver hairpins found beneath the skull of a female burial (case 40). In the next two rooms

The Roman Theatre, Fiesole

the most outstanding exhibits are a tombstone of a type specific to the Fiesole region (5C BC) decorated with an illustration of a funeral meal, a dance and an animal combat, several pieces of black Etruscan buccheroware dating from the 6C BC (cases 43 and 46), and vases from Apulia in Southern Italy with refined decoration dating from the 4C BC (cases 51 and 52).

The museum also houses the Costantini Collection of red and black figure Greek vases and Etruscan buccheroware.

Also on view are the excavations conducted on the site now occupied by the museum (partial remains of murals dating from Roman times).

■ Museo Bandini

On the first floor – paintings from the 14C and 15C Tuscan School – Petrarch's *Triumphs*, a work by the Florentine School at the end of the 15C; *(left) The Triumph of Love and Chastity* and *(right) The Triumph of Time and Religion*.

■ Other Sights in Fiesole

Badia Fiesolana – *3km/2mi SW of Fiesole. Almost halfway down between Fiesole and Florence, turn right into the narrow Via Badia dei Roccettini.*
The Badia Fiesolana (Fiesole Abbey), which now hosts the European University Institute, was originally a Benedictine convent. In the 15C it was partly rebuilt in the elegant style of Brunelleschi at the expense of Cosimo the Elder, who was a frequent visitor.

The highly ornate decoration of the original Romanesque **façade★**, composed of geometric motifs in green and white marble, in a similar style to San Miniato in Florence, has been rather strangely integrated into the new façade which was left unfinished on the death of Cosimo the Elder.

San Domenico di Fiesole – *2.5km/2mi to the SW, beside the Florence road (left), just after the junction with Via Badia dei Roccettini.*
The church of San Domenico was built in the 15C and altered in the 17C; the arcaded porch and bell tower date from the latter period.

Fra Angelico took his vows here, c 1420, and spent several years in the adjacent monastery *(private)*. The church contains *(1st chapel on the left)* a delicate but vividly-coloured **painting★** representing the Virgin Mary in Majesty surrounded by angels and saints, which he painted c 1430; it was originally painted on a gold background and designed as a triptych but the various parts were brought together in 1501 by Lorenzo di Credi; *(second chapel on the right)* the *Baptism of Christ* by Lorenzo di Credi. ■

DIRECTORY

■ Useful Information ■

🖪 Via Cavour, 1, 50129 Firenze, ☏ 055 29 08 32.

Special Needs – An office, Ufficio Assistenza Disabili, is located at Santa Maria Novella railway station, ☏ 055 23 52 275.

24hr Pharmacy – At Santa Maria Novella railway station, ☏ 055 21 67 61, in Via dei Calzaiuoli 7r, ☏ 055 21 54 72 and 055 28 94 90 and in Piazza San Giovanni 20r, ☏ 055 21 13 43

Lost Property – Via Circondaria 17b. ☏ 055 32 83 942

Consulates – UK – Lungarno Corsini 2; ☏ 055 21 25 94, 055 28 74 49, 055 28 41 33

USA – Lungarno Vespucci 38; ☏ 055 239 82 76, 055 21 76 05, 055 28 02 61, 055 28 40 88

Post and telecommunications – Via Pellicceria 3 (near Piazza della Repubblica) is the office which deals with poste restante mail. At this office there is also a telephone operator service until midnight, although Florence is well supplied with card phones. There is another post office in Via Pietrapiana 53/55.

■ Transport ■

Getting there

By train: Santa Maria Novella railway station is in the city centre.

By air: Amerigo Vespucci Airport is served by airlines operating both domestic and international flights. A bus of the Slta/Ataf company ("Vola in bus") links the airport with the city centre in about 20min, stopping in Santa Maria Novella. In Pisa's Galileo Galilei Airport, the Pisa Aeroporto railway station is linked to Santa Maria Novella station in Flroence.

Getting about in Florence

Walking is by far the best solution. Florence has an ancient urban structure with narrow streets full of innumerable scooters and cars driven by Florentines who tend to be rather fast drivers. The one-way systems can be daunting if one doesn't know the city, traffic is often restricted to residents only and some car parks are also open to residents only. It is therefore a good idea to leave your car in the car parks on the outer side along the beltway, at Santa Maria Novella station, on Piazza della Libertà, Piazza Ghiberti, Piazza Beccaria and Piazza delle Murate. As car parks are expensive; it is advisable to arrive by train or, for the motorists staying in central hotels without car parks, to park the car in peripherical quarters and use public transport.

Get more information at Firenze Parcheggi, ☏ 055 50 01 994, www.firenzeparcheggi.it

Buses (street network and SUburban network)

The main routes are:

Lines 12 and 13 going from the station to the Piazzale Michelangelo

Line 7 going from the station to Fiesole, passing by San Marco

Line 10 going from the station to Settignano

Line 17 going from the station to the youth hostel (Salviatino's stop)

Line 25 going from the station to Pratolino (Villa Demidoff)

Line 37 going from the station to Galluzzo

It is recommended to consult the ATAF website full of information: www.ataf.net/

☏ 800 42 45 00 or 055 56 50 222

Taxis

To call a taxi call ☏ 055 4242, ☏ 055 4390, ☏ 055 4798, ☏ 055 4499

Car Hire

Cars can be hired at the airport or in town at one of the following agencies:

Avis, Borgo Ognissanti 128r, ☏ 055 21 36 29, 055 23 98 826, 055 28 90 10; a subsidiary of Ponte Sospeso, ☏ 055 22 07 188.

Italy by Car, Borgo Ognissanti 134r, ☏ 055 28 71 61, ☏ 055 30 04 13 (at the airport), Fax 055 29 30 21.

Europcar, Borgo Ognissanti 53r, ☏ 055 29 04 37.

Hertz, Via Maso Finiguerra 33r, ☏ 055 23 98 205.

Bicycles

Cycling is one of the best ways to see Florence and to bypass the permanent traffic congestion. Bicycles can be rented at some hotels or from **Florence by bike** (☏ 055 48 89 92, www.florencebybike.it, info@florencebybike.it) which has a range of different types of bicycle and scooter for hire in summer only and provides guided cycle tours of the city and the surrounding district during which the leader describes the points of interest.

Bikes are also available for rent at **Alinari**, via Guelfa 85r. ☏ 055 28 05 00.

■ Where to Eat ■

⊖   Budget
⊖⊖   Moderate
⊖⊖⊛   Expensive

⊖ **Nerbone** – *Stand 292* - ☎ *055 21 99 49* - ✄. This restaurant should not be missed. It is located inside San Lorenzo's market, and since1872 local salesmen have come to eat here, as well as several generations of local people, and, for quite a time now, a few curious tourists. *Lampredotto* sandwiches (tripe cooked in the Tuscan manner), soups and meats are served to eat standing up or sitting at small tables.

⊖ **Al Tranvai** – *Piazza Tasso 14r* - ☎ *055 22 51 97* – *booking essential.* In this small and simple restaurant, tables are arranged in two lines against the walls; alongside them are two long white benches, like those in old tramways. You will find a warm atmosphere, traditional Florentine dishes extremely well cooked and mostly Florentine customers.

⊖ **Trattoria Mario** – *Via Rosina 2r* - ☎ *055 21 85 50* - *trattoriamario@libero.it* - ✄ ▭. The perfect *trattoria* for a quick meal, in the heart of the city. Workers, employees and students crowd in to enjoy simple, traditional cooking. A modest restaurant with casual service and reasonable prices.

⊖ **Enoteca Fuori Porta** – *Via Monte alle Croci 10r* – ☎ *055 23 42 483* – *ifo@fuoriporta.it* – *Booking essential.* The young and enthusiastic owners of this well stocked wine bar were among the first in Florence to offer good quality wine. The menu consists of hors d'oeuvres and cold dishes do not miss the large white beans on toast *(crostini)*.

⊖ **Trattoria Gozzi** – *Piazza San Lorenzo 8r* - ☎ *055 28 19 41*. The Gozzi brothers, passionate and modest as always, run this genuine and very charming *trattoria* located in the heart of San Lorenzo market. Open only for lunch. Tuscan cooking. Fish served on Tuesdays and Fridays.

⊖ **Mario** – *Via Rosina 2/r* - ☎ *055 21 86 50* - ✄. This small *trattoria* owes its originality to its tables covered with paper tablecloths and its kitchen located in the dining room. It serves home cooking prepared with quality products in a trice. A very good management which has been operating for fifty years.

⊖ **Cantinetta dei Verrazzano** – *Via dei Tavolini 18/20* – ☎ *055 26 85 90* – *cantinetta@verrazzano.com* Small but sophisticated place with four strong points: its cooking, its wine, its desserts and its long hours. The menu offers charcuterie, round or long sandwiches *(panini)*, toast rubbed with garlic *(bruschette)*, cheese and cakes, accompanied with wine from the Fattoria di Verrazzano, served by the glass.

⊖ **La Casalinga** – *Via dei Michelozzi 9r* - ☎ *055 21 86 24* – *Booking essential.* Located a few steps away from the charming Piazza Santo Spirito, this spacious *trattoria* offers a family atmosphere where you can taste traditional

Florentine specialities, from starter to dessert. Courteous staff offering quick service in two rooms with simply-laid tables.

◉ **Palle d'Oro** – *Via Sant'Antonino 43/45r* – ☎ *055 28 83 83* – 🖩 – *Booking essential.* Not far from the lively San Lorenzo market, this wine bar was started early in the 20C by the great grandfather of the present owners. On the menu: Tuscan specialities, rice dishes, pasta or, for those in a hurry, sandwiches *(panini)* served at the bar.

◉ **Trattoria Anita** – *Via del Parlascio 2r* - ☎ *055 21 86 98* - ✎ - *Booking essential.* This simple and homely *trattoria* is popular with workers and employees at lunchtime. In the evening, it attracts mainly tourists and families. Prices remain reasonable.

◉ **Le Mossacce** – *Via del Proconsolo 55r* - ☎ *055 29 43 61* - 🖩. This tiny restaurant has a genuine and jolly atmosphere. Tables are close together so that you will easily mix with employees, barristers and magistrates from the nearby courthouse. Tasty Florentine cooking, based on natural products.

◉ **Osteria delle Belle Donne** – *Via delle Belle Donne 16r* - ☎ *055 23 82 609* - *www.osteriabelledonne.com* – *booking essential.* The unusual decoration of this restaurant makes it a place halfway between a shop selling objects from the 1950-60s and a colourful grocery shop. Both tourists and Florentines visit this restaurant to enjoy traditional cooking.

◉ **Ruth's** – *Via Farini 2* – ☎ *055 24 80 888* – 🖩 – *Booking essential.* This elegant restaurant next to the synagogue provides Kosher cooking and an opportunity to taste Jewish dishes to the strains of klezmer music.

◉ **Del Carmine** – *Piazza del Carmine 18r* – ☎ *055 21 86 01* – *Booking essential.* This restaurant offers a variety of dishes – regional specialities, national dishes and some fish dishes. In summer, if you are lucky and move quickly, you may get a table outside.

◉ **Trattoria Sostanza-Troia** – *Via del Porcellana 25r* - ☎ *055 21 26 91* - ✐ - *Booking essential.* This *trattoria* was founded in the mid-19C, and has occupied its current location since 1932. The charming owner has worked here for about fifty years and this place has become an institution. Simple atmosphere and Tuscan cuisine.

◉ **Vini e Vecchi Sapori** – *Via dei Magazzini 3r* - ☎ *055 29 30 45* - 🖩 – *Booking essential.*

Behind the Palazzo Vecchio, this tiny place, which has a very pleasant atmosphere, offers a variety of appetising Florentine dishes: *la ribollita* or tripe (including the *lampredotto*), and a selection of *crostini* (assorted cold meats and cheese). Be prepared to wait!

◉◉ **Del Fagioli** – *Corso Tintori 47r* – ☎ *055 24 42 85* – ✐ 🖩. A typical Tuscan trattoria offering good traditional Florentine dishes prepared on the premises. Unpretentious service and pleasant family atmosphere. Very relaxing.

⊝⊜ **Baldini** – *Via il Prato 96r* – ☎ *055 28 76 63* – ▦. At this trattoria near the Porta al Prato visitors are greeted with a particular friendliness in the family atmosphere. The dishes are authentic, whether local or not. This is a good place to try the traditional *Fiorentina* steak.

⊝⊜ **Trattoria Cibreino** – *Via dei Macci 122r* – ☎ *055 23 41 100* – *cibreo.fi@tin.it* ▦ – *Booking essential.* This restaurant, near the Sant'Ambrogio market, is a branch of the elegant restaurant of the same name. It is one of the most fashionable in town; the atmosphere is young and alternative but without pretension. Delicious traditional cooking and good wine.

⊝⊜ **Ciro And Sons** – *Via del Giglio 28//r* - ☎ *055 28 96 94* - ⊷. Inside the splendid palazzo Aldobrandini, in a magnificent room decorated with 18C frescoes, this restaurant offers an unexpected speciality: delicious Neapolitan pizzas baked in the wood-fired oven. A few more typical dishes with reasonable prices are included on the menu.

⊝⊜ **Il Guscio** – *Via dell'Orto 49* – ☎ *055 22 44 21* – *fgozzini@tiscali.i* – ▦ ⊱ – *Booking essential.* Situated between San Frediano and Santo Spirito, a restaurant frequented by those who appreciate typical Florentine cooking and carefully chosen wine. Dark wooden tables and attentive service make for pleasant and relaxing dining.

⊝⊜ **Enoteca Pane e Vino** – *Via S Niccolò 70a/r* – ☎ *055 24 76 956* – *paneevino@yahoo.it* - ▦. This wine bar on the south bank of the Arno combines rustic style with elegant attention to presentation. Traditional dishes enhanced by imaginative detail. Extensive wine list.

⊝⊜ **Il Latini** – *Via dei Palchetti 6r* – ☎ *055 21 09 16*. Locals and visitors find themselves side by side around the great wooden tables in this crowded restaurant, popular for its exuberant conviviality as much as for the quality of its traditional local cooking.

⊝⊜▣ **Cibreo** – *Via dei Macci 118r* – ☎ *055 23 41 100* – *cibreo.fi@tin.it* – ▦ – *Booking essential.* Not far from Sant'Ambrogio this restaurant provides traditional dishes, carefully presented with a good choice of wine. The décor is elegant and sober, the staff attentive but relaxed. Bar service next door.

In Fiesole

⊝ **India Ristorante e non solo** – *Largo Gramsci 43* – ☎ *055 59 258* – *maharaja.srl@tin.it* ▦ – *Booking essential.* If you tire of Tuscan cooking, try the contrasting flavours of Tandoori and Moghul cuisine. After visiting Florence or an evening at the Fiesole amphitheatre, treat yourself to an "alternative" meal in a different ambience.

■ Where to Stay ■

⊖ Budget
⊖⊜ Moderate
⊖⊜⊛ Expensive

⊖ **Ostello Villa Camerata** – *Viale Augusto Righi 2/4, zona Salviatino – 5km/ 3mi from the centre, towards Fiesole; bus 17 – ☎ 055 60 14 51 – Fax 055 60 13 00 – ⊠ ⋈ ⧓ – 322* beds - *Restaurant.* The view of Fiesole from this address makes it hard to believe that it is in one of the busiest tourist cities in Italy. The 15C building has been converted into a hostel with bunk beds, shared bathrooms and a restaurant.

⊖ **Ostello Santa Monaca** – *Via Santa Monaca 6 – ☎ 055 26 83 38 - Fax 055 28 01 85 - info@ostello.it - ⋈ - 114 beds.* In the heart of the Oltrarno, between Piazza San Spirito and Piazza del Carmine, a former 15C monastery houses this fine youth hostel which reflects the seriousness and professionalism of the co-operative in charge of the management. Picturesque corridors lead to the bedrooms, which can contain from 4 to 20 beds.

⊖ **Campeggio Michelangelo** – *Viale Michelangelo 80 – ☎ 055 68 11 977 – Fax 055 68 93 48 – michelangelo@ecvacanze.it – 240 sites.* This large campsite is situated not far from the city centre below Piazzale Michelangelo and next to an olive grove. It is well equipped with an open-air bar-restaurant and a mini-market for provisions. The tents and the camper-vans are positioned on terraces which descend to the bank of the River Arno.

⊖ **Ostello Archi Rossi** – *Via Faenza 94r – ☎ 055 29 08 04 – Fax 055 23 02 601 – ostelloarchirossi@hotmail.com - ⊠ ⋈ ⧓ – 97 beds.* Although a little old fashioned this a good place to stay owing to its very central location and its pleasant atmosphere. The wall paintings, the work of past visitors, are an interesting sample of contemporary urban art.

⊖ **Youth Firenze 2000** – *Via Raffaello Sanzio 16 – ☎ 055 23 35 558 – Fax 055 23 06 392 – scatizzi@dada.it – ⊠ ▣ ⌇ ⋈ ⧓ – 94 rooms.* Part hotel, part inn, this address is noted for its spacious private bathrooms and its very practical electronic keys which confer complete autonomy on the visitor. Only 15min on foot from the Ponte Vecchio.

⊖ **Hotel Orchidea** – *Borgo degli Albizi 111 – ☎ 055 24 80 346 – Fax 055 24 80 346 – hotelorchidea@yahoo.it – ⊠ – 7 rooms.* The English owner has created a quiet, family atmosphere on the first floor of this old mansion in the historic town centre. The spacious rooms have high ceilings and simple decoration. Shared bathrooms.

⊖⊜ **Residenza Hannah e Johanna** – *Via Bonifacio Lupi 14 – ☎ 055 48 18 96 – Fax 055 48 27 21 - lupi@johanna.it – ⊠ – 11 rooms.* Well placed near to Piazza San Marco, a warm welcome and reasonable price. Attention to detail shows in the books and reviews available. Breakfast is provided on a tray in the rooms.

Residenza Johanna – *Via Cinque Giornate 12* – ☎ *055 47 33 77* – *Fax 055 47 33 77* - *cinquegiornate@johanna.it* – ⊞ ▣ – *6 rooms*. A small quiet hotel appreciated for its welcoming atmosphere. The car park in the tiny courtyard (a rare facility in Florence) compensates for its isolated location (about 30min on foot from the town centre). Breakfast is provided on a tray in the rooms.

Orcagna – *Via Orcagna 57* – ☎ *055 66 99 59* – *Fax 055 67 05 00* – *info@hotelorcagna.com* - ▦ – *18 rooms*. A warm welcome awaits in this simple family-run hotel with comfortable and well maintained rooms. Bicycle hire to enable you to reach the town centre speedily.

Residenza Apostoli – *Borgo Santi Apostoli 8* – ☎ *055 28 84 32* – *Fax 055 26 87 90* – *residenza.apostoli@infinito.it* – *11 rooms*. Not far from the Ponte Vecchio stands the 14C Palazzo del Siniscalco, offering pleasant and well appointed rooms, furnished with taste and a few retro flourishes. Breakfast is served in the bedroom.

Hotel Cimabue – *Via B Lupi 7* – ☎ *055 47 56 01* – *Fax 055 46 30 906* – *info@hotelcimabue.it* – *16 rooms*. Even if you cannot afford a suite or one of the bedrooms with frescoes on the ceiling, you will enjoy the spaciousness, the remarkable furniture and the quiet family atmosphere.

Albergo Scoti – *Via Tornabuoni 7* – ☎ *055 29 21 28* – *Fax 055 29 21 28* – *hotelscoti@hotmail.com* – ♿ – *7 rooms*. The location in elegant Via Tornabuoni and the frescoes in the saloon give this Renaissance mansion an aristocratic air tempered by a hint of decadence. Small shared bathrooms.

Hotel Palazzo Vecchio – *Via Cennini 4* – ☎ *055 21 21 82* – *Fax 055 21 64 45* – *info@hotelpalazzovecchio.it* – ▣ ▦ ♿ – *25 rooms*. This hotel, near the Palazzo dei Congressi, has huge attractively decorated bedrooms. Warm welcome to tourists as well as conference participants from the management.

Albergo Firenze – *Piazza Donati 4* – ☎ *055 21 42 03* – *Fax 055 21 23 70* - *firenze.albergo@tiscalinet.it* – ⊞ ♿ – *60 rooms*. The 13C tower house belonging to the powerful Donati family has been converted into a hotel, offering welcoming public rooms and modern, functional bedrooms at a reasonable price, despite its location near to Piazza della Repubblica.

Residenze Johlea I e II – *Via San Gallo 76/80* – ☎ *055 46 33 292* – *Fax 055 46 34 552* – *www.johanna.it* – ⊞ – *12 rooms*. These two addresses are branches of a small chain of charming B&Bs offering elegance and comfort in a homely and relaxed atmosphere.

Locanda di Firenze – *Via Faenza 12* – ☎ *055 28 43 40* – *Fax 055 28 43 52* – ▦ – *6 double rooms*. Not far from San Lorenzo market, on the 3rd floor of an old mansion. A retired university professor welcomes tourists as if they were guests in his own comfortable home. An unexpected lodging offering comfort and personal attention.

Bed & Breakfast Dei Mori – *Via Dante Alighieri 12 – í 38 - deimori@bnb.it –* ▦ *– 12 rooms.* This is a welcoming B⌐ mansion, near Dante's House and the Cathedral, with a classic amᵼ created by painted headboards and attention to romantic detail. Smokıⁿᵍ allowed on the balcony only.

Hotel Fiorino –*Via Osteria del Guanto 6 –* ☎ *055 21 05 79 – Fax 055 21 05 80 – fiorinohotel@tin.it - 23 rooms.* If you are looking for a place to stay near the Uffizi, try this small family-run hotel. The large and airy rooms are plainly but suitably furnished.

Relais Uffizi – *Chiasso de' Baroncelli-chiasso del Buco 16 –* ☎ *055 26 76 239 –*

Fax 055 26 57 909- info@relaisuffizi.i – ▦ *– 10 rooms.* This is just the place you are looking for – a medieval Florentine palazzo with a welcoming and elegant ambience and a great room overlooking Piazza della Signoria for breakfast and throughout the day.

In Fiesole

Dino – *Via Faentina 239 -* ☎ *055 54 89 32 - Fax 055 54 89 34 -* ▣ *- 18 rm. - Restaurant.* Enjoy the peace and tranquillity of the hills, not far from Fiesole centre, at this simple, family-run hotel which offers well-kept bedrooms with rustic-style decoration.

Pensione Bencistà – *Via Benedetto da Maiano 4 –* ☎ *055 59 163 – Fax 055 59 163 - pensionebencista@iol.it –* ▣ *– 45 rooms.* This peaceful old town house with period furnishings is set among the olive trees. The terrace and the large garden have panoramic views of Florence and the Arno Valley.

■ Taking a Break ■

Boccadama – *Piazza Santa Croce 25/26r -* ☎ *055 24 36 40 - tony.sasa@boccadama.it* Situated in the lovely Piazza Santa Croce, this is the perfect place to have a coffee, a drink or a cold or hot meal. Pleasant decoration, courteous service, large wine cellar.

Enoteca Bonatti – *Via Gioberti 66/68r –* ☎ *055 66 00 50 - erbonatti@tin.it* The Bonatti family has maintained its cellar and its reputation here since 1934. The wine list covers the whole of Italy – some 1 000 wines including a good choice from Chianti and Brunello di Montalcino.

Piti Gola e Cantina – *Piazza Pitti 16 –* ☎ *055 21 27 04 – pigola@tin.it* Situated in the arcade of the Accademia Italiana in front of the Palazzo Pitti, this wine shop, which also sells books on wine, specialises in the great names among Tuscan wines. Service indoors at the old marble counter or out on the terrace.

Vip Bar –*Viale Giuseppe Poggi 5r –* ☎ *0335 54 17 544 (mobile).* For one of the best views of Florence, come to this bar which specialises in ice cream and cocktails and boasts a huge flower-bedecked terrace overlooking the city.

Vivoli Piero Il gelato – *Via Isola delle Stinche 7r* – ☎ *055 29 23 34* – *vivoli@mail.cosmos.it* Among the many ice cream parlours in Florence, connoisseurs would choose this little place, founded in 1930, as a good example of Italian flair. Ices to eat on the premises or to take away.

■ Going Out ■

Caffè Paszkowski – *Piazza della Repubblica 6* - ☎ *055 21 02 36*. If every café in the square has its speciality, this bar-patisserie without doubt specialises in music; every evening an orchestra plays on the terrace.

Caffè Pitti – *Piazza Pitti 9* – ☎ *055 23 99 863*. This is an elegant bar of original and modern design. It is worth spending a little time at one of the outdoor tables if only to enjoy the panoramic view of the Palazzo Pitti.

Caffè Storico Letterario Giubbe Rosse – *Piazza della Repubblica, 13/14r* - ☎ *055 21 22 80* - *giubbe.rosse@tin.it* The name derives from the enduring tradition that the waiters wear red waistcoats *(giubbe rosse)*. This literary café was frequented by Marinetti, Papini, Prezzolini, Campana, Gadda, Boccioni and Montale and many futuristic canvasses on the walls pay homage to their meetings.

Cantinetta Antinori – *Piazza degli Antinori 3* – ☎ *055 29 22 34*. Marquess Antinori invites you to his beautiful 15C mansion to taste his famous wine, including the Solaria, which has been judged the best in the world. A few vintage crus are very elegantly displayed.

Caffè Cibrèo – *Via Andrea del Verrocchio 5r* – ☎ *055 23 45 853* – *cibreo.fi@tin.it* With its coffered ceiling, its ancient furniture and its soft armchairs, this magnificent café is one of the most popular in Florence. Unfortunately, everyone knows it and most of the time you have to stand if you wish to enjoy its incomparable ambience.

Rivoire – *Via Vacchereccia 4r* – ☎ *055 21 44 12*. The great terrace looks out on Piazza della Signora with the Palazzo Vecchio and *Perseus* by Cellini. The round tables of this famous café, founded in 1862, are always crowded and this affects the price of a cup of coffee – the most expensive in Florence.

In Fiesole

Caffè al no 5 di Piazza Mino – *Piazza Mino* – ☎ *055 59 250*. This café in the main square *(no 5)* is the oldest in Fiesole, founded in 1908.

■ Entertainment ■

Florence is a city of art and music, particularly in the evening when shows and concerts are performed in the theatres. The local daily newspaper – *La Nazione* – prints the programme and starting times of all the shows in the city.

Box Office – *Via Alamanni 39r* – ☎ *055 21 08 04*. Make reservations at the Teatro della Pergola from the Tuesday before the concert. For the programmes of the other theatres – Teatro Verdi, the Teatro Comunale, the Teatro Goldoni, Musicus Concentus – look at the *Firenze Spettacolo.*

■ Shopping ■

Florentines are great traders and there is no lack of choice. Popular items include:

Stationery, in Piazza della Signoria, Via de' Tornabuoni and Piazza Pitti;

Embroidery, in Borgo Ognissanti;

Leather goods, more or less everywhere but particularly at the leather-work school (Scuola del cuoio di S. Croce);

Fashion, in Via de' Pucci and in Via de' Tornabuoni;

Jewellery, in Via de' Tornabuoni and on the Ponte Vecchio.

The walk from Piazza della Signoria to the Duomo along Via dei Calzaiuoli is rich in opportunities to pause for a drink in a bar or to buy ceramics or leather goods.

It would also be a good idea to take a look at the stalls in San Lorenzo market, in Cascine (Tuesday) and the Flea Market (Piazza dei Ciompi).

■ Events and Festivals ■

See under the heading *Events and Festivals (p. 26).*

INDEX

Director	David Brabis
Series Editor	Manuela Magni
Editorial Team	Erica Zane, Elisabetta Rossi, Sybille Bouquet, Aude de La Coste-Messelière, Juliette Hubert, Pierre Boussard, Élise Pinsolle
Picture Editor	Catherine Guégan
Mapping	Michèle Cana, Thierry Lemasson
Graphics Coordination	Marie-Pierre Renier
Graphics	Antoine Diemoz-Rosset
Lay-out	Michel Moulin
Typesetting	Sophie Rassel et Franck Malagie (NORDCOMPO)
Production	Renaud Leblanc
Marketing	Agathe Mérel
Sales	Paolo Riccardi
Public Relations	Kenol Verdoia
Contact	Michelin – Edizioni per Viaggiare
Via Vincenzo Monti, 23
20016 PERO (MI)
☎ 02 33 95 35 41 – fax 02 33 95 37 38
www.ViaMichelin.it
LaGuidaVerde@it.michelin.com

Edizioni per Viaggiare

Michelin Italiana S.p.A.
Via V. Monti, 23 – 20016 PERO
www.ViaMichelin.it
LaGuidaVerde@it.michelin.com

MANUFACTURE FRANÇAISE DES PNEUMATIQUES MICHELIN
Société en commandite par actions au capital de 304 000 000 EUR
Place des Carmes-Déchaux – 63 Clermont-Ferrand (France)
R.C.S. Clermont-Fd B 855 200 507

Published in 2004

Front cover: The Duomo (B. Pérousse/MICHELIN) – *Copy of Michelangelo's David, Piazza della Signoria* (J. Malburet/MICHELIN) – *The Ocean Fountain in the Boboli Gardens* (J. Malburet/MICHELIN) – *Ponte Vecchio* (B. Pérousse/ MICHELIN) – The Bell Tower by Giotto (Ph. Orain/MICHELIN) – *«Primavera» by Botticelli, detail* (Ph. Benet, R. Holzbachova/MICHELIN)